St. Bridget of Sweden

Francesca Maria Steele

ST BRIDGET OF SWEDEN.

St. Bridget of Sweden

※※※※※※※※※※※※※※※※※※※※※※※※※※※※

BY

FRANCESCA M. STEELE

('DARLEY DALE')

AUTHOR OF 'THE STORY OF THE ENGLISH POPE,' 'CONVENTS
OF GREAT BRITAIN,' 'ANCHORESSES OF THE WEST,'
'MONASTERIES OF GREAT BRITAIN AND
IRELAND,' ETC

WITH PREFACE BY

THE REV. G. BROWNE, D.D.

The CATHOLIC HOME LIBRARY

R. & T. WASHBOURNE, LTD.

PATERNOSTER ROW, LONDON, E.C.

MANCHESTER ❧ BIRMINGHAM ❧ GLASGOW

PREFACE

THE BREVIARY OF THE ORDER OF
ST. SAVIOUR

By REV. G. BROWNE, D.D.

THIS Breviary, recently reprinted at the expense and
for the use of the nuns of Syon Abbey, Chudleigh,
is the service book of the Brigittine Order, and
contains the psalms, hymns, and prayers used by the
Sisters in their daily offices in choir throughout the
year. It certainly deserves its title of 'most ancient,'
for it has been used by the nuns of St. Bridget since
the very foundation of the Order. It dates back to
234 years before the time of the Council of Trent, as
Simon Hörmann tells us in his preface to the edition
of 1697, and this gives it at the present day an antiquity
of 665 years. Moreover, it has not been subjected
during the course of ages to the changes which have
befallen other service books, especially the Roman
Breviary; for, with very few additions and no altera-
ations, it is the same now as it was in the fifteenth
century, when the author of the 'Mirror of Our Lady'
translated it into English for the benefit of the nuns
of Syon Abbey at Isleworth.

Most, if not all of the Orders of nuns that had been

established up to the time of St. Bridget were obliged
to use the ordinary Roman or else the Monastic
Breviary, but the Brigittine nuns have an original
office-book of their own. According to the Rules of
their Order, which St. Bridget received in a series of
revelations from Our Lord, the Sisters were commanded
to recite the Hours of the Blessed Virgin every day
with a nocturn and three lessons. They were also
bidden to ask pardon of each other publicly in choir
before Vespers for anything they might have said or
done to offend one another during the day. A Mass
of the Blessed Virgin was to be said every day, and
each Hour was to conclude with the 'Hail Mary' and a
prayer. Except for these general indications, nothing
is said in the Rule as to the order in which the
psalms and prayers were to be recited, and it was left
to Master Peter de Alvastra, a Cistercian monk and
friend of St. Bridget, to arrange the details of the office.
To him is certainly due the distribution of the psalms
in the Daily Hours, and most probably it was he who
composed or selected the hymns, as well as many
anthems and responsories. For although the nuns
are said to recite the Hours of the Blessed Virgin, yet
their service has very little in common with the
Little Office of Our Lady, for they are obliged to recite
the entire Psalter every week, a practice which is in
accordance with the primitive Roman and monastic
observance, though unfortunately it is not often
followed at the present day. Now in the Roman and
monastic offices the greatest portion of the Psalms
are recited at Matins and Vespers, the first 108
Psalms being mainly set apart for Matins, and the

remainder for Vespers. This arrangement makes Matins by far the longest of the Canonical Hours. At least twelve Psalms must be recited every day at Matins, and four or five at Vespers, if the Psalter is to be read through in a week. But the Matins of the Brigittine Breviary is very short, consisting only of three Psalms and three lessons, so that the weekly recitation of the Psalter has to be secured by having different Psalms appointed every day for the other canonical Hours, as well as Matins. The Psalms which are not included in the Daily Hours are left to be recited at certain subsidiary offices during the week, and no feast, however great, is allowed to interfere with this regular weekly recitation of the Psalter.

The feasts in the Kalendar, with few exceptions, do not cause much variation in the weekly services; but the hymns and lessons which are recited each day are made to illustrate different mysteries of the faith. Thus, the office on Sunday is devoted to the Blessed Trinity, on Monday to the angels, on Tuesday to the Creation and fall of Adam, on Wednesday to Our Lady's nativity, on Thursday to her maternity, on Friday to her sorrows at the foot of the Cross, and on Saturday to her Assumption and to her Coronation in Heaven.

The Lessons.

The Lessons at Matins are all taken from the Revelations of St. Bridget upon the glories of the Mother of God. The author of the 'Mirror of Our Lady' tells us that while St. Bridget was living in Rome, near to the Church of St. Laurence, in Damaso, she fell to wondering what lessons should be read by

the nuns in her monastery, which Our Lord had
bidden her build in Sweden.   And as she prayed,
Our Lord appeared unto her, and said, 'I shall send
thee mine angel that shall reveal unto thee the legend
that shall be read at Matins by the nuns in thy
monastery, and write thou it as he saith unto thee.'
The angel thereupon appeared unto St. Bridget, and
she wrote down the legend at his dictation in her own
mother-tongue.   Afterwards she showed it to Master
Peter, her confessor, who translated it into Latin, and
sent it to a Spanish Doctor of Divinity to be reviewed
and corrected if necessary.   Thus, concludes the
author of the 'Mirror of Our Lady,' 'after the setting
of Master Alphonsus (the Spanish Doctor)[1] is your
legend read in all places of this Order.'

THE HYMNS.

The hymns of the Brigittine Breviary are thirty-
five in number—that is, five for each day of the week.
Only three or four of these are taken from the Roman
Breviary ; the others seem to have been written by
the same person, probably Master Peter de Alvastra.
All the hymns, save three which are of different metre,
end with the two verses :

1. 'Mary, Mother of Grace,
    Mother of Mercy,
    Defend thou us from the enemy,
    And take us up to thee in the hour of our death.

2. Glory be to the Lord
    That was born of the Virgin,
    With the Father and the Holy Ghost,
    Without end.   Amen.'

---

[1] Alphonsus of Vadaterra, Bishop of Jaen.

The hymn *Ave Maris Stella* is sung every day before Vespers, and the verse beginning ' Show thyself a Mother ' is repeated thrice. There are also two other hymns in use which are not included in the thirty-five already mentioned — the hymn ' Veni Creator,' which is said at the Little Office of the Holy Ghost every Sunday, and a hymn in praise of St. Bridget, which is said or sung every day in choir after Vespers.

ANTHEMS, RESPONSORIES, CANTICLES, ETC.

Far superior to the hymns, from a literary point of view, are the numerous anthems and responsories, which are among the most beautiful features of this Breviary. Take, for instance, the following anthem, which is sung at Lauds every Friday, and which is reproduced in Latin, as well as in English, because the rhythm is lost in the translation :

' Misereatur nostri Deus altissimus,
O Mater vitæ, interveniente te, qui
Nobis humiliter sociatus est

Obediente te, et pro nobis morte
Turpissima damnatus, vidente te.'

' May the most High God have mercy on us
By means of thee, O Mother of Life, who
By thine obedience meekly became our
Fellow-man, and in thy sight was
Condemned for us by most foul death.'

These anthems and responsories are so excellently translated in the ' Mirror of Our Lady ' that I reproduce some of them to give an idea of their beauty. Where necessary, the spelling has been modernized.

Sunday at Compline. Anthem to the 'Nunc Dimittis.'

'O untouched Mother of the King of Peace, set us, thy servants, together in the healthful peace of thy Son.'

Monday. Anthem 3 at Matins.

'Lady, Mother of Joy, turn our sorrow into joy, and close us all about with joy, that we, joying, may show forth the truth of God.'

Monday. Second Responsory at Matins.

'Blessed be the earth, whose flowers fade not; whose fruit is the life of all that live,
'Giving nourishment to all mankind.'

'*V.* Forsooth, this earth is the Virgin Mother; the flowers are her works, her Son is the fruit,
'Giving nourishment to all mankind.'

Tuesday. Anthem 3 at Matins.

'Mother of health and life, save us from them that trouble us, that the shadow of death cover us not; for we spread out our hands to thy Son, very God.'

Tuesday. Third Responsory at Matins.

'O Little Maiden, unspeakably rich in a poor town, who received the Son of the High King sent unto her into the Hall of Gladness. She fed Him with desired delights, and girt Him about with the armour of power.

'*V.* This Overcomer, going again into His country, made her Queen in endless praising. Who received the Son of the High King sent unto her into the Hall of Gladness. She fed Him with desired delights, and girt Him about with the armour of power.

'Glory be to the Father, and to the Son, and to the Holy Ghost.

'She who received the Son of the High King,' etc.

The responsories always correspond in meaning with the lessons that precede them, while the anthems, as a rule, combine a verse of the Psalm to which they belong with a reference to the Blessed Virgin.

For instance, Psalm lvi., used at Matins on Thursdays, contains these verses :

> ' I will cry unto God most High :
> God hath sent His mercy and His Truth :
> They dug a pit before my face, and they are fallen into it.'

These verses are thus combined in the anthem attached to the Psalm :

> 'We have cried to God most High, and He hath sent us His Truth by Mary, His chosen Spouse. And they that delved a pit for us are fallen therein themselves.'

The office of Lauds on Friday contains four canticles from the Old Testament, while two more are recited at Vespers the same evening. This arrangement is rather displeasing, and it is noteworthy that a rubric directs that these canticles are never to be sung on double and semi-double feasts. The order of the Roman Breviary seems preferable, which appoints one of these canticles to Lauds on each day of the week, but an arrangement similar to that of the Brigittine Breviary occurs at Sunday Matins, both in the Ambrosian and in the Monastic Rite. A very pleasing feature of this office is that the fifth and last Psalm at Vespers is always the 147th. This is one of the seven Alleluia[1] Psalms, or Psalms of Praise, which

---

[1] So called, because the title 'Alleluia' is prefixed to each of them in the Bible.

come at the end of the Psalter. The three last
Alleluia Psalms are, as is well known, sung every day
at Lauds, but Vespers is quite as much an office of
praise as Lauds, hence it seems fitting that the last
Psalm at Vespers should, in the Brigittine Breviary,
always be a Psalm of Praise.

SOURCES OF THE BRIGITTINE BREVIARY.

The Hours of the Brigittine Breviary are framed
after the model of the Hours of the Roman Breviary.
There are, however, some exceptions. Compline has
only three Psalms, agreeing in this respect with the
Monastic Breviary, whereas the Roman Breviary has
four. Again, the Saturday office bears a close re-
semblance to the Little Office of Our Lady, which is
of monastic origin. Then, too, the latter part of
Prime is recited in the chapter-house, and on Saturday, after Lauds, the servitors who are to do duty for
the week have to come into choir to ask a blessing upon
their work, exactly as it is laid down in the Rule of
St. Benedict. Doubtless these monastic traits in the
Breviary are due to the fact that Master Peter, who
had so much to do with its arrangement, was a
Cistercian monk.

While most of the hymns, anthems, and responsories
are original, there are some which are taken from the
Roman Breviary. Thus the anthems of the Wednesday
office are taken from the Feast of Our Lady's Nativity,
those of the Thursday office belong to the Feast of
the Circumcision of Our Lord, while the anthems
for Saturday come from the office of Our Lady's
Assumption.

The Swedish origin of the Order is shown by the presence of certain Swedish saints in the Kalendar. It must not be forgotten also that the Rule of the Brigittine Order is based, to a certain extent, upon the Rule of St. Augustine. Three feasts are assigned to him in the Kalendar, and perhaps a comparison with the Augustinian office-books might bring to light other resemblances.

Sufficient has been written to give the reader a description of a Breviary which should be dear to English Catholics, since it was used by the nuns of Syon Abbey before the Reformation, and, though that community was driven into exile, it never ceased to be English, and its members have now returned, as did the Israelites after the captivity, to sing again those same songs of Syon, not in a strange land, but in the land of their birth.

DECLARATION

In accordance with ecclesiastical decrees, the author of this book makes the following statements:

If in the course of the work the title of 'Saint,' 'Martyr,' 'Blessed,' 'Confessor,' or the like, is ascribed to anyone not actually canonized or beatified by the Apostolic See, it is done on mere human authority.

If, moreover, any miracle, or vision, or other extraordinary fact with regard to such is related, the reality of such fact rests solely upon ordinary historical testimony.

In regard to the sanctity of persons or their marvellous deeds, it is not the intention or wish of the author to presume to anticipate the judgment of the Church.

In these and all other respects, therefore, the work is unreservedly submitted to the authority of the Holy See.

FRANCESCA M. STEELE.
('Darley Dale.')

June 1, 1909.

WORKS CONSULTED

Acta Sanctorum.   Boll.

Die Heilige Birgitta.   K. Krogh Tönnung.

La Vie de Ste. Brigitte de Suède.   La Comtesse de Flavigny.

History of Syon Monastery.   Aungier.

Revelationes Sanctæ Birgittæ Sueciæ.   Roma, 1606.

Vita Sanctæ Birgittæ.   Roma, 1606.

Vita Sanctæ Catherinæ Sueciæ.   Roma, 1606.

Vita Patris Petri Olafson.   Harleian MSS., fol. 612*f*, 291*b*, coll. 160.

Vita Sancti Nicolai Episcopi Lincopensis.   Harleian MSS., fol. 612*f*, 291*b*, coll. 160.

Wanderings of Syon.   Manuscript at Chudleigh.

Valuable manuscript notes collected from Harleian MSS.

Gesammelte Nachrichten über die einst bestandenen Kloster der Heilige Birgitta.

Manuscript notes of (Miss) Mary Howitt.

Diarium Wazstense in Fant's Rerum Suecicarum.

Lives of the Fathers, etc.   Butler.

Histoire Générale de l'Église, par l'Abbé J. E. Darras.

Catholic Europe.   W. Barry.

European History.   Lodge.

CONTENTS

INTRODUCTION

THE life of a saint who played so important a part in the history of her time as St. Bridget of Sweden seems to require a slight sketch of the state of Europe, of the Church, and especially of the Papacy, during the period in which she lived, 1303-73, as a prelude to her biography, and as a help to the understanding of her work and character.

She lived throughout the greater part of the fourteenth century. Now the watchword of that century was 'Reform.' In 1311, when Clement V. consulted William Durandus as to how to hold the Council of Vienna, he answered, 'The Church ought to be reformed in its head and in its members.'[1] The reformation of the clergy, and especially of the religious Orders, was the leading idea of the time among thoughtful churchmen; it was, as we should say, 'in the air.' It rang through all the fourteenth century, and its octave note was struck at the Council of Pisa in 1409.

As this idea of reformation developed, it became twofold: there was the reformation desired by loyal Catholics, the friends of the Church, and there was, later on, the so-called reformation desired, and un-

---

[1] W. Barry, 'Catholic Europe.'

fortunately accomplished only too successfully, by the enemies of the Church, those schismatics and heretics known as the Protestant Reformers.

It is sometimes said that St. Bridget was a pioneer of the Reformers. If by this is meant that she belonged to the Catholic Reformers, the true sons of the Church, it is true; but no one would have detested more the heresies of Luther, Huss, Calvin, and Knox, and the rest of the Protestant Reformers, than the Swedish seer had she lived in their time.

Laxity in the observance of monastic discipline, especially with regard to the precept of Holy Poverty, had crept into most of the religious Orders, and a reaction had set in among the Franciscans, and had led to quarrels between the two parties, among the Friars Minor, of the 'spirituals' and the 'conventuals.' The spirituals went to the length of maintaining that a friar had no right of property even in his own food; but they were themselves split up into several parties. While St. Bridget was still a child, Pope John XXII. published his celebrated constitutions, condemning the Fraticelli and their communistic ideas. Then arose another dispute, when the General of the Franciscan Order and our William Ockham, known as the 'invincible doctor,' also a Friar Minor, maintained that Our Lord and His Apostles possessed nothing, either individually or in common; they and their followers belonged to a school of philosophic thought called the Nominalists. A year later John XXII. published a second decree pronouncing this to be heresy, and, as the authors of it persisted in teaching it, he excommunicated them, and they went over to the party of the Emperor, Louis of Bavaria.[1] Notwithstanding these decrees, the echoes of these disputes were heard when St. Bridget was in Italy, in 1350-73, pursuing her great work of bringing the Popes back from Avignon to Rome.

Europe was agitated all through the first half of this century by the struggle between the Papacy and the Empire. The historic quarrel between Philip le Bel and Boniface VIII. took place before St. Bridget was born, so we need not deal with it here, especially as we have had occasion to allude to it in the text. To still further complicate matters, on the death of the Emperor Henry VII. there were two rival Emperors, Frederick the Handsome, who had himself crowned at Bonn on the same day as his opponent, Louis of Bavaria, had himself crowned at Aix—November 25, 1314.[2] Pope John XXII. was for Frederick, and when he succeeded Clement V., in 1316, he summoned Louis to plead before his court, and when he refused to come, excommunicated him.[3] The struggle between the Empire and the Papacy lasted until Louis's death in 1347; the Fraticelli went over to the side of the Emperor after the publication of the decrees condemning their doctrines. Louis of Bavaria was a greater enemy to John XXII. than Frederick Bar-

---

[1] L'Abbé Darras, 'L'Histoire Générale de l'Église,' vol. iii.

[2] St. Bridget lived during the reigns of the following Popes : Benedict XI., 1303; Clement V., 1305; John XXII., 1316 ; Benedict XII., 1334; Clement VI., 1342; Innocent VI., 1352; Urban V., 1362; Gregory XI., 1370.

[3] Lodge, 'European History : Close of the Middle Ages, 1273-1494.'

barossa had been to Adrian IV. in the twelfth century.
Louis braved the sentence of excommunication passed
upon him, and even presumed to set up one of the
Fraticelli as Antipope under the title of Nicholas V.,[1]
whom he sacrilegiously crowned in St. Peter's, and
the new Antipope reciprocated the compliment by
crowning Louis. Prince Colonna had the courage to
publish the sentence of excommunication on the walls
of the Vatican, and the Antipope submitted, and
begged for pardon at the feet of the Pope.[2]

Jean de Cahors, who took the title of John XXII.,
was a Gascon, and the second of the French and
Avignon Popes; his predecessor, Clement V., had transferred the Papal Court from Rome to Avignon in
1308. This city then belonged to the King of Naples;
but Rome was so torn by the dissensions of the
Colonna and Orsini, who tyrannized over the people,
that it had become a very turbulent place to live in:
the brawls between these two rival princes and their
retainers continually disturbed the peace, and the
Popes had often had to take refuge elsewhere. The
anarchy which prevailed led to the establishment of a
government of thirteen, with the Captain of the people
and Senator at its head.[3] Clement V. obtained this
power for life, and in 1308 he decided to move the
curia to Avignon; and as most of the Cardinals then
were Frenchmen, this step met with their approval,
for Avignon was a beautiful city, and a pleasanter
place of residence than Rome at that period.

[1] The title of Nicholas V. was subsequently (1447-55) borne
by an Italian Pope, the founder of the Vatican Library.

[2] Darras, 'Histoire Générale.'

[3] Lodge, 'European History, 1273-1494.'

At this time every large city in Italy was either a republic, or had a despot ruling over it. When Clement V. went to Avignon with his Court, Rome was left deserted and forlorn, and there was no restraint upon the unruly citizens, for as long as the Popes were there, they could to a certain extent control them. Petrarch in 1336 saw with grief the squalid surroundings of mediæval Rome, in striking contrast with the grandeur of its classical monuments, and twice he besought Benedict XII. to return to it.[1]

In Florence the struggle between the Guelphs and Ghibellines lasted all through the fourteenth century, the Guelphs being always on the side of the Popes, the Ghibellines always opposed to them. In Northern Italy a great struggle was going on between the two great maritime cities of Venice and Genoa, who had been rivals for power in the Levant ever since the Crusades; they were reconciled in 1350-55, Venice being triumphant, and Genoa never regaining her former prestige.

The terrors of the age in Italy were added to by the marauding bands of freebooters called Condottieri which devastated the country; of these, the principal was that of the celebrated White Company under Sir John Hawkwood, whose lawless excursions struck terror into the hearts of the unfortunate peasants. Later on Pope Urban VI. enlisted Hawkwood's services against the Antipope Clement VII.[2]

Spain was the scene of the struggle between the Christians and the Mussulmans; the Moors had overrun the peninsula, and all Europe was watching with

[1] Barry, 'Catholic Europe.'
[2] Lodge, 'European History, 1273-1494.'

anxiety this struggle. Benedict XII., who succeeded John XXII. in 1334, settled the quarrel with Louis of Bavaria, and did his best to make peace between Philip VI. of Valois, King of France, and the nephew of Philip-le-Bel, and Edward III. of England. Philip had ascended the throne on the death without issue of his uncle Charles IV., the third son of Philip-le-Bel, and Edward III. most unjustly claimed the throne of France on behalf of his mother, Queen Isabella, the daughter of Philip-le-Bel ; but as the Salic law prevailed in France, Isabella had no legal pretensions to a throne she was debarred from ascending. Benedict succeeded so far in making peace as to obtain a truce for a year between the two Kings, but the war broke out again under his successor, Clement VI., and was still raging when Innocent VI. came to the throne in 1352.

Naples and Sicily were ruled over during the beginning of the fourteenth century by the good King Robert the Wise, who was succeeded by his grand-daughter, the beautiful but much-maligned, and certainly worldly, Joanna I., called by Petrarch the 'Light of Italy' and the 'Jewel of the World,' and known all over Europe as 'the sweet Queen.'[1] Her story is one of the most romantic in history, and she is often described as the Neapolitan Mary Stuart. She was a friend of St. Bridget's, and also of St. Catherine's, and they both visited her Court, which was the most cultured and refined in Europe, as Joanna was a highly accomplished woman and a generous patroness of all the arts. The most learned

[1] Rotteck, 'Joanna die Erste,' vol. i., pp. 1-23.

and greatest literary men of the age, notably
Petrarch and Boccacio, frequented her Court. Her
first husband, Andrew of Hungary, to whom she
was married for political reasons when a child, was
murdered some years after their marriage, and
Joanna was accused by her enemies of being an
accomplice in this crime; but there seems to have
been no foundation for this calumny, and Pope
Clement VI. was convinced of her innocence. She
sold Avignon, which belonged to her, to this Pope in
1348 for 80,000 gold florins.[1] Her reign was a very
disturbed one: her implacable enemy Louis, King of
Hungary, the elder brother of her first husband,
Andrew, invaded her kingdom to revenge his brother's
death, and her life was a series of struggles to retain
her throne. When Urban VI. came to the throne, he
treated her very unfairly, and this drove her to take
the part of the Antipope Clement VII., whereupon
Urban excommunicated her. This has prejudiced some
French Catholic historians against her, and whether
or no she had any part in the murder of Andrew of
Hungary will always be a disputed point; the Italians
look upon her almost as a saint.

The state of Norway and Sweden and the Court of
Magnus II. is described in the text, so we need not
say more about it here.

Clement VI. (Pierre Roger), a Benedictine Pope,
ascended the throne in 1342. He loved pomp and
magnificence, but he was generous and amiable. He
succeeded in getting another truce signed between
England and France, but it was not observed, and

[1] This is equal to £60,000 of our money.

the war continued. Louis the Bavarian, who for thirty years now had troubled the peace of the Popes, pretended to submit to Clement, but in 1344 he convoked a Diet at Frankfort, which he induced to protest against the ambition of the Pope, who then resolved on the deposition of the Emperor in favour of Charles of Luxembourg. Charles was elected in 1346, and in the following year ascended the throne under the title of Charles IV., when Louis died, and the long contest between the Papacy and the Empire ended.

In 1342 there was a great outbreak of the Black Death, or plague, which raged in England, France, Germany, Italy, and Scandinavia, and then Clement's best qualities showed themselves in his great charity and fatherly care for the sufferers.

It was at this time that the Flagellants reappeared in Rome, where they made a pilgrimage to the tombs of the Apostles to appease the Divine wrath, and with their fanatical processions, gave a great deal of trouble to both the Church and the State.

When Innocent VI. came to the throne, in 1352, Germany was the only European Power that was quiet.[1] In Spain Peter the Cruel was pursuing his policy of wholesale assassination to subdue the power of the nobles, and scandalizing all Europe by the murder of his own brother, and by other cruelties and crimes. France and England were still fighting, and in Italy there were as many little wars as there were cities. Both France and Spain despised the authority of Innocent, and in 1362 he died, worn out with age

_____
[1] Darras.

and infirmities. At the conclave which followed his death Cardinal Hugh Roger, a brother of Pope Clement VI., was elected to the Chair of Peter, but he refused the honour, and the Abbot Guillaume Grimoard was elected in his stead. He took the title of Urban V. Although a Frenchman, he sympathized with Rome, now left a widow, and considered Avignon only a temporary seat of the Papacy, which he desired to move back to Rome.

He instituted some wise reforms, especially with regard to simony, then very prevalent in the Church. This he dealt with very severely, as it merited. He was said by Cardinal Talleyrand[1] to be ' powerful both in word and deed,' and was famed for his charity and justice. Although opposed by the Sacred College, consisting then mostly of French Cardinals, he determined to return to Rome, and on April the 30th, 1367, he left Avignon, and sailed with a large escort from Marseilles. He entered Rome on August the 24th, and was received with the greatest joy by the citizens. The Emperor Charles IV. met him in Rome, and received the Imperial Crown from his hands. He remained in Rome till 1370, when he was forced to return to Avignon. St. Bridget predicted his death if he yielded to the pressure of circumstances and left Rome, but he disregarded this warning, and died suddenly of an unknown malady on December the 19th of the same year. He died at Avignon in the odour of sanctity, and was succeeded by Cardinal Pierre Roger de Beaufort,

---

[1] Cardinal Hélie de Talleyrand was a contemporary of St. Bridget, 1301-64, and a friend of Petrarch. He played an important part in the elections of four Popes.

the last of the French Popes, a nephew of Clement VI. He took the title of Gregory XI. This Pope was induced, by the eloquence of St. Catherine of Siena, to transfer the Papal See from Avignon to Rome in 1377. Thus St. Bridget did not live to see the work accomplished for which she had striven so long and so well, for she died in 1373.

ST. BRIDGET OF SWEDEN

CHAPTER I

ST. BRIDGET'S CHILDHOOD

'Who shall find a valiant woman? Far and from the utter-most coasts is the price of her.'—PROV. xxxi. 10.

In the beginning of the fourteenth century there stood in the province of Upland, in Sweden, the fine old castle of Finstad. It was built of wood, after the Swedish custom of that day, but it was well protected by stone walls, ditches or fosses, and palisades; it stood in beautiful country, surrounded by forests of pines and firs, and watered by lakes of various size and a river.

The nearest town was three miles away, and the immediate vicinity of the castle was very lonely and silent, the dark fir-trees lending a touch of mystery to the scenery, which was not without its effect upon the saint, whose early years were passed within those red-painted wooden walls of her ancestral home.

At this time Sweden was divided into nine pro-vinces, of which Upland was one. Birger Person was the Governor of Upland, and the highest nobleman in the province; he exercised all the rights of a sovereign,

1

and was himself of royal blood, being related to the reigning King of Sweden, while his wife, Ingeborg, was also a connection of the Swedish royal family, and both of them were descended from the holy King Eric of Denmark.

These were the parents of St. Bridget of Sweden, usually described by her biographers as a princess. Her father, Birger, was probably the richest man in Sweden; he was well educated, and very learned in law and jurisprudence; moreover, he was very pious. He confessed every Friday, and communicated every Sunday; he gave large sums of money to churches and monasteries, and made many pilgrimages, especially to Rome and St. James of Compostella, in days when pilgrimages were fraught with danger to life and limb, and afforded ample means of mortification, even when the proverbial peas were not placed in the shoes of the pilgrim. He had a large retinue of knights and men-at-arms, of huntsmen and servants, but he refused to possess any slaves, as many of his rich contemporaries still did.

His wife Ingeborg was a very devout and holy woman, and although her high position obliged her to wear magnificent clothes, and to live in great state, yet she was humble of heart, and did not scorn domestic duties, and brought up her children most piously.

Just before St. Bridget was born, at the end of 1302, Ingeborg was very nearly drowned in a storm while cruising with her husband and some of the royal family round the coasts of Sweden; she was washed overboard by the waves, and rescued by Duke Eric, the eldest brother of the King. Birger had already four children—two sons and two daughters—when this fifth child was born to him, and was named after her father Birgitta, which in Swedish means 'Birger's daughter'—the French Brigitte, the English Bridget. The following year Ingeborg had another little daughter, who was named Catherine.

We are told that St. Bridget at first appeared to be dumb, for till she had completed her third year she could not speak a word, and then she suddenly began to talk quite clearly and distinctly—not as little children usually prattle. As soon as the child was old enough to hear Mass, Ingeborg took her daily with the other children to the large chapel adjoining the castle, where every morning, before a large congregation of retainers and servants assembled with the family, the chaplain said Mass.

Very early in their lives Ingeborg taught her children to pray, and to go to confession, and do penance for their faults; they were also accustomed to accompany their mother when she visited the poor and sick in their homes. She took care to have them educated to fit them for their future position in life, but she paid especial attention to their spiritual training, in which the court chaplain and the provost of the cathedral, a great friend of Birger's, took part.

Ingeborg had a very great love for Our Lord, and an intense devotion to His Passion; she was also rich in the virtues of humility, patience, obedience, charity, modesty, and simplicity. She was greatly given to prayer, and we cannot doubt that the future saint owed much to her mother's example and training.

When the child Bridget was only seven years old she had her first vision. She woke one night, and saw on an altar which stood opposite her bed Our Blessed Lady standing dressed in glistening robes; in her hand was a precious crown. She called to Bridget to come to her, and when the child sprang out of bed and hastened towards her, Our Lady asked: 'Would you like to have this crown?' Bridget nodded, and then felt the crown placed on her head; she went back to bed, but she never forgot the vision.

When she was ten years old her mother took her one day to church to hear a sermon preached, probably by a Dominican friar, who was giving a kind of mission to the people; he was an eloquent preacher, and the sermon made a great impression upon the child. It was upon the Passion of Our Lord, and it filled her with great grief and sympathy. That night she woke and saw Our Lord looking as if He had just been crucified. She asked Him who had so ill-treated Him, and He answered: 'Those who despise Me and forget My love.'

From that time Bridget always had a great devotion to the Passion of Christ, which was from henceforth the centre of her interior life; it was the subject of many of her revelations: again and again she returns to it in the course of them—indeed, she seems from that day to have lived almost constantly in the presence of Jesus crucified, and she was rarely able to meditate upon His sufferings without tears.

Two years later, in 1314—that is, when Bridget was

about twelve years old—Ingeborg fell dangerously ill, and died with her weeping children standing round her bed; she was buried with great pomp in a chapel in the Cathedral of Upsala. Bridget and her sister Catherine were then sent to their Aunt Catherine, their mother's sister, the wife of Canute Jonson, the Marshal of East Gotha, who lived in the Castle of Aspenæs, on the borders of a lake in Westmanland.

The children here led a similar life to that to which they had been accustomed at Finstad. Their uncle, the Marshal, occupied a very high position, and lived in princely style; their aunt was a very pious woman, who brought up her nieces wisely if strictly, and taught them all the domestic duties women were then expected to perform, especially spinning and church embroidery.

Two legends are told of Bridget while living at Aspenæs, and as they both illustrate the manners of the age, we shall quote them. Catherine Jonson seems to have kept a sharp eye on her nieces, and one night, after they had gone to bed, and were supposed to be asleep, she went into their room, and found Bridget out of bed kneeling at the foot of a crucifix. Catherine not approving of this precocious piety, as she deemed it, and thinking it was a capricious fit of devotion that was best dealt with summarily, called for a rod, but as she raised it to strike Bridget it broke before it touched the child. 'What is the meaning of this? What are you doing?' asked Catherine, and Bridget meekly answered that she was praising Our Lord. So her aunt, after consulting the holy Bishop of Skara, by his advice allowed this child, who was so unlike other children, to follow her devotions undisturbed.

Another day all the ladies-in-waiting and young girls—Catherine's companions—were gathered together in the large salon of the castle working: some were spinning, some were making clothes for the poor; others were engaged in church embroidery, others making tapestry. Bridget was sitting in the embrasure of a window at her embroidery-frame embroidering a vestment for the parish church. The child was unable to fulfil her task to her own satisfaction, and prayed to Our Lord to help her. Presently Catherine, going round the room to see how her maidens were progressing, saw a beautiful unknown lady standing by Bridget's side, who disappeared without leaving any trace of her presence, except that the fruit and flowers on St. Bridget's frame were most beautifully executed. 'Has anyone helped you?' said Catherine. 'No,' replied the child, for she had seen no one; but her aunt, convinced that she had had help from the mysterious stranger, treasured the work as a most precious relic. Bridget was now growing into a beautiful young girl, though she is described as very small and frail, with a wealth of golden hair, which almost veiled her, an aquiline nose, and a small mouth with thin lips. Several portraits of her have been reproduced at various times, but they differ very much from each other. On the whole, the above description of her would seem to be fairly accurate, and her biographers are agreed that she was small and fair. The Poor Clares in Rome are said to possess a robe which belonged to the saint, the size of which confirms the tradition that she was a little woman. Although she was now only fourteen, she began, according to the custom of her country and epoch, to go into society. We learn that she was always bright and cheerful, amiable and charming. Before she had completed her fifteenth year her life at Aspenæs was to come to an end, for Birger had met two young noblemen, Ulf, Prince of Nericia, and his brother Magnus, whom he had accepted as husbands for his daughters Bridget and Catherine, and he sent for them to return to Finstad to prepare for the marriage of Bridget and Ulf.

CHAPTER II

ST. BRIDGET AS WIFE AND MOTHER

'The heart of her husband trusteth in her: she will render him good and not evil all the days of her life.'—PROV. xxxi. 11.

IT happened that St. Bridget's father, Birger, had had occasion to travel into East Gotha on business, and had there been entertained by two brothers, Ulf, or Wolf, Prince of Nericia, and his younger brother, Magnus, sons of Gudmar, the former Seneschal, or Governor, of the province. These two young sons of Odin were orphans living in their castle of Ulfasa; they were very rich, and were also tall, strong, handsome youths of seventeen and eighteen. They had been educated by some Cluniac monks, who had a monastery in the neighbourhood, and were fervent Christians, well instructed in their religion.

Following the custom of the age and country, Birger, while at Ulfasa, arranged that the brothers should become his sons-in-law, and marry his two young daughters. Bridget, who, we are told, would rather have died than be married, and who wished to be a nun, though she had not yet decided on her vocation, acting upon the advice of her confessor, obeyed her father's wishes and submitted to his will. Catherine, on the contrary, was delighted at the prospect, and consented willingly enough, and as soon as the girls reached Finstad they were bidden to prepare their wedding garments, and within the same year Ulf and Bridget were married.

Ulf, who was only eighteen, came to Finstad to fetch his bride accompanied by a princely retinue, who, before they entered the castle, disarmed and placed their weapons in Birger's hands, while he invited them to eat bread and salt, the pledges of their safety while under his roof. Then the little Bridget, with a jewelled crown upon her head, was led into the great hall of the castle to meet the tall bridegroom. When this first meeting was over she retired to put on her riding-habit, and then, accompanied by her maids-of-honour, with her father by her side on horseback, she rode to Ulfasa with her bridegroom, followed by the wedding-guests and a large escort of armed men. The marriage took place in the chapel of Ulfasa, after which Bridget's beautiful golden hair was hidden under a kind of cap, then worn by married women in Sweden.

The wedding festivities were kept up for several days, during which the poor, as well as the rich, were entertained, and the bride waited on all her guests. After this Birger returned to Finstad, leaving his little daughter in her new home.

There are few more edifying pictures of married life in history than that given us of Ulf and Bridget by her old biographers. Their high rank and position, their riches and their youth, all might have tempted them to lead useless, selfish, frivolous, and worldly lives; but, on the contrary, their manner of living was most exemplary in every way. Ulf had plenty to do in governing his province, in administering justice, in cultivating his large estates, in rebuilding his castle as he did; moreover, he was a soldier and a keen sportsman, very fond of hunting, which then, after fighting, was the great occupation of the upper classes.

St. Bridget, for her part, was occupied in entertaining her husband's and her own relations, the neighbouring clergy, travellers, and pilgrims, for it is clear that she and her husband kept what we call 'open house.' She delighted in making clothes for the poor and embroidering vestments for churches; she superintended her gardens, and introduced foreign fruits and flowers and vegetables into her country, which at that time was only half civilized. She overlooked her household, the kitchens, the dairy, the brewery—no part escaped her supervision; and how she found time for it all is surprising.

Above all, she spent several hours daily in prayer, in visiting the sick and tending them, and in relieving the wants of the poor. Every day, before she sat down to dinner, she entertained twelve poor people, and waited upon them herself, and every Thursday she knelt down before them and washed their feet and kissed them, in imitation of Our Blessed Lord on the eve of His Passion.

At her own table she was most abstemious, fasting often besides on the appointed fasts of the Church. Her handsome goblet, long preserved in the Brigittine convent of Mariboo, never contained anything but water.

In the practice of austerities she led the way,

teaching her youthful husband to follow in her footsteps in this respect. She frequently slept on the
floor in Lent and Advent, and on vigils. They both
belonged to the Third Order of St. Francis, and said
their office together. They heard Mass daily, went to
confession every Friday, and to Holy Communion
every Sunday.

Thus, in fulfilling the duties of their state in life, in
works of charity, and in penitential exercises, did they
pass the first two years of their married life. Then
civil war broke out in Sweden, and Ulf had to leave
his young wife and go and fight, and assist his father-
in-law, Birger, who was also engaged in this campaign,
and Bridget was left at home to pray for their safe
return, and learn the anxiety of a soldier's wife and
daughter in time of war. Her constant prayers for
Ulf's safety were granted, and after his return their
happy, useful life was resumed until after Birger
Person's death, when Bridget was called to Court by
Magnus II., King of Sweden.

While living thus quietly at Ulfasa, St. Bridget had
many learned priests among her friends. The holy
Bishop Nicholas Hermanson, of Lincoping, whose
canonization was afterwards asked of Leo X., but
prevented by heresy breaking out, was one of these
friends. He was a great almsgiver, and was most
generous to the poor and sick; he was also a contem-
plative, and practised great austerities, and, as we
shall see later on, was once rebuked by St. Catherine
for indiscretion in this respect. The canons of Lincoping were also on friendly terms with the young
Prince and Princess of Nericia, and one of these,

Canon Matthias, or Master Matthias, as he was called, was their confessor and director, and had a great deal to do with the development of St. Bridget's character.

Master Matthias was a very learned man; he translated the Pentateuch into Swedish. St. Bridget begged him to translate the whole of the Bible into her native language, but he died at Stockholm when the plague was raging there in 1350, before he had completed this task. Of him St. Bridget learnt Latin while living at Ulfasa, and she took great interest in his Biblical studies. Yet the Comtesse de Flavigny[1] says they were never on such intimate terms of friendship as have existed between other saints and their directors. At this time of her life obedience was not easy to Bridget, though she had a profound reverence for priests, and gladly performed the severe penances and austerities Master Matthias imposed upon her. One of her faults, which she strove hard to overcome, was the pride and prejudice of her rank, which made it repugnant to her to look upon the common people as her equals, as in some regards they were not. Human nature is very much the same in the twentieth century as it was in the fourteenth, when we see even a canonized saint finding it easier to wash the feet of the very poor than to avoid haughtiness in her demeanour to those beneath her in rank.

In 1328 the saint lost her father, the Seneschal of Upland, who was buried with almost regal pomp in the Cathedral of Upsala. By his death Ulf and Bridget succeeded to some of his estates, and Ulf soon

[1] 'La Vie de Ste. Brigitte de Suède,' par la Comtesse de Flavigny, p. 41.

after became Seneschal of Nericia, to which post he was elected in 1330.

Ulf and Bridget had eight children, four sons and four daughters. Charles, the eldest son, who in due course succeeded his father, was a great soldier, but of a fiery disposition, pleasure-loving, religious by fits and starts, and a great source of anxiety to his parents. His father idolized and spoiled him, and reproached himself bitterly for so doing when he saw the ill-effect of his weakness. Charles married three times, and died at Naples in the prime of his life on his way to the Holy Land.

Birger, the second son, was always quiet and devout. He accompanied his mother and his sister Catherine on their way to the Holy Land, and ultimately, on the death of Charles's son, became Seneschal of Nericia, and died a holy death at Vadstena.

Benedict, the third son, was a Cistercian monk at Alvastra, and died in the monastery there after a long illness. Gudmar, the youngest son, was always delicate. He died at Stockholm while studying there.

Martha, the eldest daughter, made an unhappy marriage, and on her husband's death became chief lady-in-waiting to Queen Margaret, then a little girl of eleven, who grew up to be a great Queen. Under her government the three kingdoms of Norway, Sweden, and Denmark were united into one.

St. Bridget's second daughter was the celebrated and beautiful Catherine of Sweden, honoured as a saint, and, it is said, actually canonized, the companion of her mother in all her travels and pilgrimages after Ulf's death, the co-foundress of the Order of St. Saviour, and first Abbess of Vadstena.

The third daughter was Ingeborg, who became a Cistercian nun in the convent at Risaberg, where she was educated, and died young. The youngest child, Cecilia, at whose birth Our Lady is said to have appeared to St. Bridget and saved her life, was twice married, and died a widow in the monastery at Vadstena.

The Bishop of Lincoping, Nicholas Hermanson, as a young man, before he was appointed to his See, acted as tutor to the elder children.

If in the above account of St. Bridget's married career we have emphasized its regular, devout character, it would not be a true picture of it if we did not also say that, in spite of the supernatural favours she enjoyed even then from time to time, and notwithstanding the deep spiritual and interior life she led, she was also her husband's constant counsellor and frequent companion in his journeys to Stockholm when called thither on State business to attend councils, or to other distant parts of his estates where his presence was required. On these occasions the Prince of Nericia travelled in state, as became his high rank.

St. Bridget encouraged and helped Ulf in his studies of the laws of his country, and if she did not take part in his hunting expeditions, she had to entertain his guests on their return from the hunt; so that their life, especially as their children grew up, was by no means dull or monotonous. In fact, the marvellous part of this home life of our saint was the way in which she combined the austerities of the cloister with the duties of a princess living in the world, and yet not of it.

CHAPTER III

ST. BRIDGET'S LIFE AT COURT

'She hath made for herself clothing of tapestry : fine linen and purple is her covering.'—PROV. xxxi. 22.

ABOUT the year 1335 a great change occurred in the life of St. Bridget : she was called to leave her home and reside at Stockholm in the royal palace. The King of Sweden, Magnus II., was then only nineteen, and was just married by proxy to Blanche, daughter of the Count of Namur, who was then a mere child, and Magnus wanted someone to act as Grand-Mistress of the palace at once, and to watch over his young bride when she arrived.

He immediately turned to Bridget, whom he venerated as a saint and loved as the daughter of his faithful subject, Birger, who had loyally supported him and fought on his side in the recent civil war. St. Bridget would fain have declined the invitation, but after much prayer and consideration she knew the call came from God, and decided to obey it and undertake the arduous duties, which, moreover, involved the breaking up of her own home.

Her eldest daughter, Martha, was married, much against St. Bridget's will, to a wild, immoral nobleman named Sigfried Ribbing, whom she speaks of as 'the

15

Robber' in the Revelations. Ulf, for the first time in
his life, had grieved his saintly wife by arranging this
marriage, which, as far as family and money went,
was a good match, but St. Bridget foresaw it would
turn out unhappily, as it did.

Her two elder sons were still under the tuition of
Nicholas Hermanson. The third son, Benedict, she
now sent to the Cistercian monastery of Alvastra, near
Vadstena, to be brought up by the monks, whom he
eventually joined. Gudmar, the youngest, who was
delicate, went with his mother to Stockholm to be
educated there. Catherine and Ingeborg were sent to
school with the Bernadine nuns at Risaberg, and little
Cecilia, the youngest of the family, to the Dominican
nuns at Skening, though it wrung her mother's heart
to part with her.

When all these arrangements were made, St.
Bridget took up her duties as Grand-Mistress of the
palace at Stockholm, and soon found they were no
sinecure. The King, though possessing some charming
qualities, was frivolous and extravagant, pleasure-
loving and selfish; his finances were in great disorder,
and to increase his revenue he laid heavy taxes on the
people. St. Bridget soon saw Magnus was a weak
character, and set herself, when Blanche came to the
Court, to try and form the young Queen into a woman
capable of guiding her imprudent and worldly husband.
Blanche, who was a mother before she was fifteen,
was as greedy of luxury and pleasure as Magnus, but
hers was a stronger nature than his, and she was
pious. She soon became greatly attached to St.
Bridget, who was a second mother to the child-

Queen, separated so early in life from her own parents.

The saint was powerless to restrain the extravagance and self-will of the young Sovereigns, although they loved and venerated her, and showed their respect and affection publicly by asking her to be godmother to the little Prince Eric, the heir to the Crown.

St. Bridget's supernatural gifts and her austerities were known in the palace, and no doubt were a subject of Court gossip in mediæval days, when religion played a larger and a more important part in the lives of even worldly people than it does now. It was no secret in Stockholm that the fragile and still young Grand-Mistress of the palace, who is said to have looked like a fairy queen, wore hair-cloth under her beautiful Court robes. It was known that she chastised her body to blood with disciplines, that she fasted rigorously, and spent many hours of the night, as well of the day, in prayer.

Her visions were talked of openly, and it was whispered that already she had worked miracles. Had she not once saved Ulf from drowning by her prayers when human aid was in vain? Had not her supernatural sense discovered the relics of St. Louis in a neglected chest, where the Queen Blanche, who had brought them to Stockholm, had left them and forgotten them? St. Bridget caused them to be placed in a costly shrine on an altar, and the Queen, as a reward, gave them to her, saying truly that she was more worthy to possess them than herself.

All this made Bridget's influence very great, but it did not avail to control the extravagance and worldliness of the young King and Queen, for all her counsels—and she did not spare them—were disregarded, and she began to feel that she had sacrificed her own home life and the care of her family in vain. After several years of Court life, the death of her son Gudmar gave her an opportunity of withdrawing from her post as Grand-Mistress for a time. She was naturally just then disinclined for society, and wished to live in retirement from Court functions and gaiety.

Accordingly, she decided to make a pilgrimage with her husband to Drontheim, where the relics of St. Olaf of Norway were kept in the cathedral under the care of the Dominican Friars. This saint at that time was the most popular saint in all Scandinavia.

The Prince and Princess of Nericia made this pilgrimage with a large escort of mounted men and many servants, and porters carrying litters, and grooms with saddle-horses, though Ulf and his wife more often walked than rode, notwithstanding the fact that the way was difficult and dangerous. We read that St. Bridget, small and frail as she was, boldly led the way over the mountains and across the trunks of trees which formed rough bridges over the rivers, encouraging the others by her zeal.

On her return from Drontheim she followed the Court to Akersbourg, on the west of Stockholm; but finding she could do nothing to check the extravagant worldliness of Magnus and his child-wife, she resolved to make a series of pilgrimages with Ulf, instead of returning to Ulfasa, which would constitute a regular breach with the King and Queen,

and she wanted to leave a door open at Court, so
that she could return if ever her presence could be
beneficial there.

In pursuance of this plan she and Ulf set out,
intending to make St. James's shrine at Compostella
the ultimate goal of their pilgrimage. Bridget longed
to go to Rome and Jerusalem, but it was not considered wise for Ulf to go so far from his province
and from his duties of Seneschal. This time they
both adopted the regular pilgrim's dress of the period,—
that is, they wore a brown habit or frock of coarse
serge, with a tippet trimmed with shells, and a large
wide-brimmed hat; they carried pilgrims' staves, and,
laying aside all signs of their rank, resolved to
observe certain counsels of perfection. They started
in the autumn of 1341 with a large company of monks
and secular priests, of mendicant friars and pilgrims
of both sexes. They first visited the shrine of the
Three Kings at Cologne, then the tomb of St. Martha
of Tarascon, and then the grotto of St. Mary
Magdalene at Ste. Baume, on the top of a wild
mountain in Provence, near St. Maximin, one of the
most celebrated places of pilgrimage in Christendom.
Here they heard a Dominican friar preach a pane-
gyric on this saint, the patroness of his Order, which
still has charge of this shrine. Finally, the pilgrims
arrived safely at Compostella, another most celebrated place of pilgrimage in mediæval days.

During their return through France, Ulf was taken
most seriously ill at Arras, and moved to the house
of one of the canons of the cathedral; he grew worse,
and his life was despaired of, and as the end seemed

near, he was anointed by the Bishop of Tournay.
St. Bridget meanwhile was suffering bitterly at the
prospect of losing her beloved husband in a foreign
land in the prime of his life, for he was well under
forty. She spent her time in nursing Ulf, and praying for his recovery if it were God's will; and then
it was that she had a vision, in which St. Denis, the
patron saint of Paris, appeared to her, and told her
Ulf would recover, and that she should one day visit
Rome and Jerusalem.

Ulf implored God to give him a few more years to
live, promising that if He would hear his petition he
would leave the world and spend the rest of his days
in a monastery. God heard the prayers of this
devout and holy couple, and Ulf recovered. True to
his resolution, made when at the point of death, he
now determined to become a Cistercian monk at
Alvastra, where he already had a son, and was well
known. This was about the year 1340, when Ulf
would be well under forty. He went to Alvastra, and
begged his friend the Prior to admit him as a
postulant, and the monks willingly consented to
receive one so distinguished and so holy; but before
he could leave the world he had all his affairs to set
in order, to resign his position as Seneschal, to pro-
vide for the management of his estates, to settle the
future of some of his children, and get his wife's leave.
All this took time, and it seems to have been three
years before he actually entered the monastery as a
postulant.

His two elder sons, Charles and Birger, were then
married, and his second daughter, Catherine, married

Edgard, the Seigneur of Eggardsnæs, just before Ulf retired from the world.

St. Bridget, who would have become a nun, but was not yet certain of her vocation, went with her husband to Alvastra, and was accommodated with very modest apartments inside the precincts of the monastery, but outside the canonically enclosed part, with one servant—a proceeding which at first caused scandal to the Subprior, Father Peter Olafson, who afterwards confessed that he had allowed himself to murmur at a woman being allowed to live at the monastery contrary to all precedent.

This Subprior of Alvastra afterwards became one of St. Bridget's directors, and continued in that capacity for thirty years; he was also entrusted to write down all her Revelations, and translate them into Latin.

Ulf only lived a year after he entered the monastery; he appears to have been clothed only just before he died, but it is certain that he did receive the habit, and was buried in it in the Cistercian monastery at Vadstena, near Alvastra, with none of the pomp and grandeur to which his rank as Prince of Nericia entitled him, but with all the simplicity of a Cistercian monk.

He appeared to St. Bridget soon after his death, and asked her to have Masses said for a year for his soul, which was in Purgatory, expiating certain sins, the chief of which were that he had been too fond of hunting; that he had idolized and spoilt his son Charles; that he had been too severe in judging a certain person, and less merciful than he ought to have been by prolonging his exile ; that he had been negligent in making sufficient provision for his wife and children, and for all these offences he was now suffering. He begged St. Bridget to give away things he had loved too much, such as his horses, and some of his silver and golden cups, which he wished her to give as chalices to churches—all of which she faithfully promised and performed. She relates this appearance of her husband in one of the books of her Revelations.[1]

[1] 'Revelationes Extravagantes,' cap. lvi. This book was called 'Extravagantes' because the Revelations contained in it were omitted when Father Peter of Alvastra divided the original celestial Revelations into eight books, and then collected these.

CHAPTER IV

ST. BRIDGET AT ALVASTRA

'She hath opened her hand to the needy, and stretched out her hands to the poor.'—PROV. xxxi. 20.

AFTER the death of Ulf, St. Bridget lived for two years, from 1344 to 1346, in a poor, modest little dwelling in the outer court of the monastery at Alvastra, with one servant to wait upon her. To one who for forty years had lived in castles and palaces, surrounded by state and luxury, a greater contrast could not have been offered; but, not content with this change of environment, she now gave herself up to a life of such terrible austerity that her biographer, Archbishop Birger of Upsala, could not conceal his surprise that so frail and delicate a woman could endure such heavy penances. Not satisfied with wearing hair-cloth under her other garments, acknowledged, as it is, to be the severest of bodily mortifications, she tied cords so tightly round her waist and knees that every movement caused her pain; she gave up the use of linen, then recently introduced into Sweden, and wore only coarse rough clothing, instead of the beautiful dresses suited to her high rank which she very properly had worn while living in the world.

28

She fasted upon bread and water four days in the week, in addition to the fasts of the Church and those of the Franciscan Order; on Fridays she drank vinegar.[1] She suffered for some time from temptations to gluttony while thus fasting, the Devil making her long for the dainty dishes and delicate food which she had been accustomed to have placed before her at Stockholm and in her own home at Ulfasa, till Our Lord heard her humble prayers for help, and removed this temptation. On Fridays, that she might share in the sufferings of her heavenly Spouse, she used to drop the burning wax from the candles lighted before the altar in the chapel of the monastery on to her bare arm. She always assisted at the canonical hours said by the monks, and if driven by the extreme cold of a Swedish winter to take refuge in a warmer part of the monastery, she recited the Psalter there. She frequently slept on the cold flagstones, with her arms extended in the form of a cross.

She deprived herself of water to assuage her thirst to such an extent that she could scarcely speak, and then Master Matthias did interfere, and ordered her to modify her severity in this respect. But for some time her directors allowed her to continue practising all her other austerities, and then, as might have been foreseen, she fell ill, and they forbade her going into such extremes.

To St. Bridget's naturally proud, self-willed temperament it was probably easier to endure any amount of bodily mortifications self-inflicted than to submit her will to another, but she showed that she had

[1] Flavigny, p. 86.

learnt to crush down self by meekly obeying her spiritual masters. She consented to take hot baths instead of cold when they were prescribed by the doctor, and she was ordered to indulge in this, which she considered a luxury, by Master Matthias and the Prior of Alvastra.

These two now acted as her directors, but as she was too far from Lincoping to see Canon Matthias often, she now went to confession to Father Peter Olafson of Skening, whom we shall in future speak of as Father Peter, to distinguish him from the Prior of Alvastra, formerly Subprior of the same monastery.

Father Peter of Skening was so holy a man that his canonization was asked of Pope Leo X., but his cause was stopped by the Protestant Reformation. He is said to have been an exceedingly helpful confessor. Filled with spiritual sweetness himself, he knew how to impart comfort and counsel to others, and it was believed that a special grace, in an unusual degree, was vouchsafed to him while administering the Sacrament of Penance.

He accompanied St. Bridget when she went to Rome and on her other pilgrimages, and for many years—indeed, during the whole of her residence in the Eternal City—he acted as procurator in her house, and as director to her and her household, which he ruled, as will be seen later on. Many miracles were reported of him. Two pretty little incidents which happened when he was a child of tender years are mentioned in his biography. As a baby he loved to be out in the open air, and would lie and look up at the blue sky, and cry when taken indoors. When he was three years old, and using a stick as a hobby-horse, he rode off out of the house into a wood, and was lost for three days, and when found by a shepherd quite happy sitting under a juniper-bush, he said 'he was in Rome.'

He began to practise great austerities at a very early age, that he might share in the Passion of Christ; he chastised his body with the discipline, wore chains and horse-hair ropes, and when assaulted with temptation, rolled himself on thorns in summer, and stood in cold water in winter.

From his boyhood he had a great faith in the Blessed Trinity, and a great devotion to the Three Persons yet One God. Though well educated, he scorned rich benefices and dignities offered him, but he accepted the office of governing the House of the Holy Spirit at Skening, which the principal citizens begged him to fill. Here he contented himself with poor food and humble clothing, and spent the rest of his means for the benefit of the poor people, suffering from various infirmities, who were in this hospital, and for others in the streets, to whom he cheerfully ministered, for he was most charitable. He continued in this office until one day St. Bridget came to see him at Skening, and asked him to become her director, and go with her to Rome, according to Our Lord's command, revealed to her in one of her visions.

St. Bridget, after being allowed by her directors to practise all these excessive austerities, was now in obedience to them to restrain her zeal, and mortify her will instead of her body—often a much harder task.

Having now described the hardships of her penitential life at Alvastra, we must say something about the spiritual favours she enjoyed, which far more than compensated her for all her penances. As we have seen, she was favoured by visions from her childhood, but at Alvastra the gift of contemplation in its highest degree was bestowed upon her, and she lived in an almost constant state of mystical recollectedness in God. She was frequently rapt in ecstasies, during which the revelations for which she is so famous were made to her. One day at Alvastra, while she was praying, she felt herself rapt into an ecstasy, and then she saw some luminous clouds open, and from the midst of them she heard a voice, saying, ' Woman, listen to Me.'

Fearing it was an illusion of the Devil, she rose immediately, and, hastening to the confessional, made her confession, and told her confessor exactly what had just happened to her, and then, after receiving Absolution, went to Holy Communion. A few days later she had a similar experience, and again heard the voice calling to her. This time also she doubted if it might be an illusion, and once again she sought her confessor, and humbly laid the matter before him.

The same thing occurred a third time, and she heard the voice say, ' Woman, listen to Me; I am the Creator of all things. Know that I do not deceive thee, and that I do not speak to thee for thyself alone, but for all Christians. Go to Master Matthias: he knows Holy Scripture from the first word to the last; he knows how to discern the Spirit of Truth and the spirit of lies, for he has experienced the struggle, and

he has conquered through My help. Reveal to him
what I say to thee. Thou shalt be My spouse; thou
shalt see spiritual things, and thou shalt penetrate
celestial secrets. My Spirit shall live with thee until
thy death. He who speaks to thee is the Word, born
of the Virgin, who has suffered, who died for the
salvation of all souls, who rose again from the dead,
and ascended into Heaven.'

St. Bridget was well versed in mystical theology:
she knew there are various kinds of visions, that some
come from God, some from the Devil, some from the
imagination of the visionary; she knew the signs of
true visions, one of which is absolute deference to the
opinion of the ecclesiastical Superior to whom they
are submitted, and without daring to decide for
herself if the voice she had heard did indeed
come from God, she went, as it bade her, to Master
Matthias, and with great humility laid the matter
before him.

Master Matthias, who had great experience in such
subjects, recognized at once that it was no illusion of
the Devil which had deceived his penitent, who was
so truly humble, and who, so far from being proud of
the Divine favours she had received, deprecated them,
and judged herself as wholly unworthy to receive
them. He therefore ordered her to believe in the
reality of her communications with Our Lord, which
became frequent, and she was called to enjoy to a
certain degree the sight of her heavenly Spouse,
though, being a living woman, she was unable to
perceive, as a pure spirit does, the heavenly things
that were shown to her. With her interior eyes she

saw these visions; with her interior ears she heard the Voice speaking to her: her soul was raised to supernatural things, while her body remained on earth. They were no dream; she was awake and watching when they happened to her, though the faculties of her external senses appeared to be suspended.

'I am Thy God,' said Our Lord to her on one occasion, 'and I will entertain thee without parables and enigmas. My Spirit shall teach thee to see, to hear, and to feel. Thy heart shall be My heart. Honour My Father. Love Me, obey My Spirit, give honour to My Mother, venerate all My saints.'

'Lord, how wilt Thou deign to live with a poor miserable widow?' cried the saint.

'If I have chosen thee,' said Our Lord, 'it is not because thou surpassest other of My friends in merits, or even that thou canst be compared to them. It is because I have so willed it. Humble thyself, and trouble thyself only concerning thy sins.'[1]

On another occasion Our Lord asked her whom He had deigned to call His spouse if she desired to be rich or poor, and she replied she would rather be poor, becauses riches hindered her from serving Him.

Then He asked if she preferred the human joys she had known to those of the Spirit, which she now enjoyed, and she answered that she blushed at the thought of past enjoyments, and that she would rather die than know them again. The spiritual joys could not be compared with them.

'My Spouse,' said Our Lord, 'in order to prepare

---

[1] 'Revelationes Extravagantes,' cap. vi.

thyself for that spiritual marriage which God enjoys in a chaste soul, do not allow thyself to be alienated from My love by thy attachment to thy family or property. Chastise with joy such of thy members as have offended Me, for My mercy cannot act against My justice. Submit thyself to others unless their will is contrary to reason, or to the salvation of thy soul. Abandon to Me thy free-will without any reserve, as My Mother did. Even on account of this spiritual union thou must be humble. My grace will make thee grow and bear fruit. A great number of souls shall owe their life to thee. But thou must work with Me if thou wouldst rest in My arms. Thou hast merited that I should have care of thee when, at the death of thy husband, thou didst put thy will into My hands. I love thy soul with an infinite love.'[1]

St. Bridget had now given up everything to Our Lord except the ring which Ulf had given her, but she felt she must break this last link with the past, and she took it off, answering those who blamed her for this final sacrifice by telling them that Ulf's ring held her to the earth, and that now she intended to do without ring or husband.

Sometimes, when the saint was caught up into realms beyond human intelligence, Our Lady appeared to her and instructed her, drawing her, as it were, under the folds of her mantle. 'Come, my daughter,' said the Blessed Mother of God, 'hide thyself under the mantle of my humility. It protects from the tempests—that is to say, from the insults and opprobium of the world, which are only wind.'

[1] Flavigny, pp. 93, 94.

One day St. Bridget went to Father Peter, now the Prior of Alvastra, and, kneeling at his feet, said to him: 'These are the orders of Christ, Brother Peter: Collect the Revelations which the Word addresses to you by the mouth of a woman. You will translate them into Latin, and for every letter you will receive not gold or silver, but an incorruptible treasure.'[1]

The Prior did not answer. He doubted whether it was the voice of God or an illusion, and, going to the church to deliberate over it, he decided from humility that he would not undertake the task, reputing himself unworthy to do it. Then, as is recorded in the Revelations, he was struck down as with a blow, and deprived of his bodily senses and power of moving, though his intellect remained clear. The monks, finding him lying prostrate on the ground, carried him to his cell and put him on to his bed, and he lay the greater part of the night in a semi-conscious state.

Then the thought occurred to him that perhaps he thus suffered because he had refused to obey the revelation made to him through St. Bridget, and humbling himself in his heart, he told Our Lord that he was willing to obey and write all the saint should tell him, and immediately after his strength returned to him, and he got up and went quickly to Bridget, and offered to write down all the Revelations that were made to her. For thirty years he translated and wrote all the Revelations, and an account of all the visions the saint had from that time till her death. He was not a good Latin scholar—at least, he did not write classical Latin—but Our Lady told St. Bridget

---

[1] 'Revelationes Extravagantes.'

that his words were more pleasing to her than the Latin of worldly men.

We are told that Father Peter suffered constantly from terrible headaches, and while St. Bridget was at Alvastra he asked her to pray for him, that if it pleased God, he might be cured. She did, and then Our Lord appeared to her, and told her to go to Father Peter and tell him that he was healed. She obeyed, and from that time for thirty years he never suffered again from headaches.[1]

When St. Bridget had been several years at Alvastra, enjoying the solitude and seclusion of the place, Our Lord one day ordered her to go back to the Court of Magnus II. at Stockholm, not as lady-in-waiting or Grand-Mistress of the palace, but as counsellor to the King, almost as a prophetess, to warn him of the disasters which were coming upon him and his kingdom in consequence of his wickedness.

St. Bridget was plunged into grief at this command, which was most distasteful to her, knowing, as she did, how fruitless her former mission at Court had been, and she cried to her Divine Master to know what she should say to Magnus when she got to Stockholm.

' Appear before him, and I will speak by thy mouth,' said Our Lord; and St. Bridget obeyed.

---

[1] 'Revelationes Extravagantes,' cap. cix.

CHAPTER V

'She hath opened her mouth to wisdom, and the law of clemency is on her tongue.'—PROV. xxxi. 26.

Before we follow St. Bridget into Sweden in her character of prophetess, we will pause to say a little about her Revelations, which once enjoyed almost as much popularity in Sweden as 'The Following of Christ.' The first printed edition was not issued until 1492, at Lübeck, nearly 120 years after the death of the saint. It was in Latin, and there have been no less than twenty-two Latin editions published at different times.[1]

Translations of some of the Revelations have been published in French, German, Dutch, Italian, and English; the first four books were translated into English by a Brigittine monk, Richard Whitford, author of the beautiful Jesus Psalter, and were published in 1531. There is an American edition of some of them, which was published in 1873. Richard Whitford was formerly a Fellow of Queen's College, Oxford; he called himself 'the wretch of Syon,' and was driven into exile at the Reformation.

[1] They were approved by Gregory XI. in 1377, and again by Urban VI. in 1379. See *Boll.*, October, vol. iv., p. 372.

Perhaps it is unnecessary to say that the Revelations, though they have been approved by some of the Popes, are not of faith. It will be as well to quote what Alban Butler says of the Revelations, for he takes a very prudent view of them:

'Nothing,' he says, 'is more famous in the life of St. Bridget than the many revelations with which she was favoured by God, chiefly concerning the sufferings of Our Blessed Saviour, and the revolutions which were to happen in certain kingdoms. It is certain that God, who communicates Himself to His servants in many ways with infinite condescension, and distributes His gifts with infinite wisdom, treated this great saint and certain others with special marks of His goodness, conversing frequently with them in a most familiar manner, as the devout Blosius observes. Sometimes He spoke in visions; at other times He discovered to them hidden things by supernatural illustrations of their understandings, or by representations raised in their imagination so clearly that they could not be mistaken in them. But to distinguish the operations of the Holy Ghost and the illusions of the enemy requires great prudence and attention to the just criteria or rule for the discernment of spirits. Nor can any private revelations ever be of the same nature or have the same weight and certainty with those that are public, which were made by the prophets, to be by them promulgated to the Church, and confirmed to men by the sanction of miracles and the authority of the Church.'[1]

[1] 'Lives of the Fathers,' etc., by Alban Butler, vol. ix., October 8.

Cardinal Lambertini, afterwards Pope Benedict XIV., is also quoted by Butler as saying that 'the approbation of such revelations is no more than a permission that, after a mature examination, they may be published for the profit of the faithful. Though an assent of the Catholic Faith be not due to them, they deserve a human assent, according to the rules of prudence, by which they are probable and piously credible, as those of Saint Hildegarde, St. Bridget, and St. Catherine of Siena.'[1]

Butler concludes by saying that if her Revelations have rendered St. Bridget famous, it is by her heroic virtue and piety that she is venerable to the whole Church.[2]

No one well versed in English or German mystical writings would ever suppose the Revelations of St. Bridget to be written by an English or a German writer. Their mysticism is essentially Swedish in character: the dark pine forests, the wild snow-storms, the terrible gales of Upland, the cold winters, and those characteristically blue evenings of Sweden, all left their impression on the mind and soul of St. Bridget, and have coloured her writings. This is obvious to any student of the Revelations, and does not in any way detract from their value.

The orthodoxy of the Revelations, or of parts of them, has frequently been called in question, both during the lifetime of the saint and afterwards. They were defended by her contemporaries, some of whom were very illustrious men, as Master Matthias and

---

[1] See Lambertini's 'De Canonizatione Sanct.,' 1, 2, c. 32 n., ii.
[2] Butler, vol. ix., October 8.

Bishop Nicholas Hermanson. She herself gave them
to many learned theologians to examine, and they
unanimously decreed that it was the Spirit of Truth
that spoke in them.

Copies were sent to Pope Gregory XI. to examine,
and a committee of Cardinals and priests arrived at
the conclusion[1] that they contained nothing to justify
suspicion, but rather much that was holy and not
inconsistent with Divine inspiration.

During the process of St. Bridget's canonization
under Urban VI., the Revelations were again strictly
examined by many learned men, and approved by
him. Again, in 1391, Boniface IX. praised them in
his Bull of Canonization, published in the second year
of his reign. When the Council of Constance was
sitting from 1414 to 1418, the Revelations were again
attacked, and a controversy arose concerning them,
and gave occasion to the celebrated John Gerson,
Chancellor of Paris, and a member of the Council, to
write his well-known treatise on ' The Discerning of
Spirits'; but he reserved his judgment (very wisely)
concerning the Revelations, though the fact that this
Council confirmed the canonization of St. Bridget, at
the request of the Swedish Ambassador, told in favour
of the Revelations.

At the Council of Basle, 1431 to 1443, a fresh dis-

[1] St. Catherine and Father Peter of Skening, and the Prior
of Alvastra, sent them to the Pope, and he gave them to
Cardinals de Luna, Mons. Major, and de Acrisolio; Martin de
Salvo, doctor-of-law; the Archbishop of Pampeluna, a learned
Dominican Master of the Sacred Palace; John of Spain; and
Alphonsus, Bishop of Jaen, to examine (*Boll.*, October, vol. iv.,
p. 372).

pute occurred concerning their orthodoxy, and the Order of St. Saviour was attacked also, not altogether unjustly; for some abuses had arisen in some of the houses, and a complaint was sent to the Council in writing, denouncing the double monasteries of monks and nuns of the Order, and alleging 123—some say 150—errors in the Revelations. Consequently, the Lady Abbess and the Confessor-General of Vadstena, Father Gervinus, and one brother Laurence were summoned to Basle to bring all the documents relating to the Revelations, and to defend their holy foundress. Father Gervinus wrote an explanation of the disputed points.

All this roused great interest in ecclesiastical circles, especially in Sweden, and a meeting of all the Scandinavian Bishops was convened at Wordingbury, and the Order was not only successfully defended, but highly praised for the excellent work done by its priests for the Church, especially in the pulpit and confessional.[1]

The Confessor-General of Vadstena then demanded that a committee should be appointed to examine the Revelations, and report upon them to the Council then sitting at Basle. This also was done, the president of the committee being no less a person than John Torquemada, afterwards the famous Cardinal of that name. He took St. Bridget's part entirely, for he had a great reverence for her, and zealously maintained the inspiration of the Revelations, which he said were not only the writings of a true saint, but were in harmony with Holy Scripture and the pro-

[1] See *Boll.*, October, vol. iv., p. 373.

phets, and with the teaching of the Church. The rest of the Committee and the Council itself agreed with this opinion.

The Revelations were divided into eight books by Alphonsus, the holy Bishop of Jaen; the ninth book was collected and arranged by Father Peter, of Alvastra, and is called the 'Extravagant' Revelations, simply because it does not form part of the original eight books, some repetitions from which are to be found in it. The 'Extravagant' Revelations are less mystical and less devotional than the other books, and perhaps more interesting, and contain also much about the rule and constitutions of St. Saviour.

The nine books are extremely long; they make in the Latin edition, including a short commentary on most of the chapters, a thick quarto volume, and there is a good deal of repetition in them.[1]

Sometimes the chapters are cast in the form of a colloquy between Our Lord and His spouse St. Bridget; sometimes the colloquy is between His Blessed Mother, the Queen of Heaven, and His spouse St. Bridget. Some chapters consist of meditations or contemplations on the Passion of Our Lord, and these, in the opinion of the present writer, are by far the most beautiful parts. The description of some scenes in the Passion, given by Our Lady to Bridget, where she tells the saint how, at the sound

[1] It is thought by many commentators that if St. Bridget had written the Revelations herself, instead of giving them to Father Peter of Alvastra, and Alphonsus of Jaen, to translate, they would have been simpler and better (*Boll.*, October, vol. iv., p. 376).

of the first stroke of the scourge, she fainted and remained unconscious, till He, her most beloved Son, all torn and bleeding from the lash, was unbound from the pillar and led away, is told with the most touching simplicity; and most beautiful is that chapter where Our Blessed Lady tells the spouse of Christ how she fainted again on Mount Calvary when she heard the first stroke of the hammer, as His enemies nailed Him to the Cross.

The introductions to many of the chapters are a kind of prose hymn of praise to Almighty God, or to the Most Holy Trinity, and these are also very fine. Every detail of Our Lord's Passion is revealed to the saint, and set forth by her more fully than in the Holy Gospels, but always consistently with them.

Many incidents in St. Bridget's life, and in the life of St. Catherine and other contemporaries, are related in the course of the nine books. Sometimes the saint prophesies evils about to come upon Magnus or his country unless the King reforms; sometimes she sees in vision certain persons-then living in sin, or lately dead, punished for their sins. Very frequently the Revelations are denunciations of the vices of the age, and contain terrible threats against persons then alive. The saint is especially severe in her warnings to priests, Bishops, and other even higher ecclesiastical dignitaries, for she was no respecter of persons, and did not scruple to mention anyone, however highly placed, to which she believed a message was sent, if not by name, yet in such terms that he was easily recognized by his contemporaries.

Sometimes the Revelations are very mystical, as

when Our Lady gives spiritual advice to St. Bridget, under the metaphor of clothing, when each garment has a mystical meaning: the cloak, for instance, is faith, the under-tunic is contrition, the tunic hope, and so on.

A great part of the work concerns the Order which Our Lord had ordered her to found: the whole of the rule, the size and construction of the monasteries, the place where the first house was to be built, the habit and every detail concerning the government of the Order, the number of monks and nuns in each convent —all were revealed to her, and are written in the Revelations.

The Revelations were brought to England in 1373, and became celebrated there; they were approved by the Oxford and London doctors, and were especially expounded by Richard Lavingham, a Carmelite, and Thomas Stubbs, a Dominican, who wrote upon them between 1375 and 1381.[1]

Sometimes in the course of these nine books pretty legends are related, which relieve the monotony of them, like illustrations. We shall conclude this chapter by translating one of these stories.[2] There was a certain Cistercian in the monastery at Alvastra named Gerechinus; he was of great sanctity, and passed most of his days and nights in prayer, and was favoured with visions. He was once told by his Abbot to go and work in the bakehouse; but not being accustomed to this kind of work, he knelt down before a picture of Our Lady on the wall, which he was

---

[1] *Boll.*, October, vol. iv., 'Vita S. Birgittæ.'

[2] 'Revelationes Extravagantes,' p. 55.

accustomed to venerate, and said: 'Dearest Lady, the Abbot commands me to labour with the bakers. Thou knowest that I know nothing about baking, nevertheless I will do thy will.'

To this Our Lady answered: 'Do what you have hitherto done; I will serve for thee in the bakehouse.'

And so it was done, and those in the bakehouse knew not who was working with them, but thought it was Brother Gerechinus, who remained fixed in prayer in the church.

CHAPTER VI

ST. BRIDGET AS PROPHETESS

'And there was at that time a prophetess who judged the people.'—JUDG. iv. 4.

KING MAGNUS II. was a weak, pleasure - loving monarch, easily led astray, and he had surrounded himself with young, foolish courtiers, whose only claim to his favour was that they flattered his vanity. His extravagance was so great that, in spite of the heavy taxes he laid upon the people, whom at the beginning of his reign he had emancipated from slavery, his debts were enormous, and he neglected to pay them; moreover, the Queen increased his financial difficulties by her prodigality towards her brothers.

Besides all this extravagance, Magnus had fallen into very great sin, for which he had been excommunicated by the Pope; but he had impiously disregarded this sentence, and had presumed to hear Mass. His people were now on the verge of open rebellion against him, as they were so disgusted with his conduct, and the burdens he had laid upon them pressed so heavily.

To this gay, frivolous, and licentious court had St. Bridget now to return, at Our Lord's command, as she believed, to rebuke the King and Queen, who

42

received her most kindly, and thus rendered her task more difficult. Very different was her appearance this time from her former entry into the palace as Grand-Mistress of it. Then she was attired in splendid robes, as beseemed a Princess; now she wore the humble dress of a poor widow, a gown of grey burrel (a coarse kind of flannel or homespun), and a long black veil, probably arranged like a nun's over a white binder; for many costumes of nuns are adaptations or copies of the mediæval widow's dress in the country in which their Order was founded. She was as much changed inwardly as outwardly. Then she was a happy wife and mother; now she was a widow and alone. She did not hesitate to perform the mission upon which she had come. She came as a prophetess, and as such she announced to the King and Queen and nobles the anger of God against them, and the judgments that were coming upon them all, in no measured terms, speaking often in the same mystical language she uses when describing the visions she had had of the Divine wrath which was about to descend upon Sweden.

The King was terrified, and her words began to take immediate effect upon him. He consented by her advice to publish a letter in which he undertook to introduce various reforms, among others, to exempt from taxation all labourers who should go back to the plough and till the soil; for many had refused to work, and there was danger of a famine in consequence. He also acknowledged that he had done wrong to debase the coin of the realm, and to transform the taxes, levied in a moment of necessity, into a perpetual impost. The saint made him further promise to administer justice equitably, and choose counsellors and ministers from among the wisest men of the kingdom.

All this, coupled with the King's zeal in following St. Bridget's advice, angered many of the nobles against her, and it can well be imagined that the inspired prophetess, who scrupled not to denounce them all as worldly and wicked, frivolous and vicious, was by no means popular at court, but was looked upon as fanatical, if not as mad.

The Bishops and clergy were not exempt from her censures. She had a vision in which she thought God told her to speak to the Bishops of the Seven Churches of Sweden, as St. John the Evangelist spoke to the Seven Churches of Asia. To the priests she prescribed a rule of life which was full of wisdom. She did not address her terrible denunciations to any Bishop or priest in particular, but left it to each individual conscience to decide to whom they referred.

She spoke also to the religious Orders, to whom, as to the friends of Our Lord, she was greatly attracted, and where any relaxations of primitive discipline or any abuses had crept into a monastery, she was sent for to exhort the inmates to repentance.

The Dominican and Franciscan Orders were now among the most influential in Sweden; the Dominicans were especially popular, and she became a friend of their convents in Stockholm, Skara, Sigtuna, Skening, and Calmar, and her influence spread to their Norwegian foundations.

The Skara convent was most exemplary in its

observance of the Dominican rule, which in its primitive simplicity is very strict. There ' abstinence was the rule and fasting the custom.' The Fathers had a magnificent church, which St. Bridget loved to people with the Dominican saints, which the Order had already given to the Church; and every time she entered this monastery we are told that she felt that Our Lady's protection promised to St. Dominic in his life was spread especially over Skara.

At the convent of Sigtuna,[1] which was built on a more magnificent scale than was altogether consistent with holy poverty, while the music was very ornate, St. Bridget reproached the Fathers very severely and so successfully that the Prior recalled the convent to the practice of the Holy Rule in all its primitive strictness; nevertheless, some of the community were incredulous of the Revelations of the saint, and rebelled against her counsels, and it is said that all these perished miserably. This may have been a strange coincidence, but in those days it was considered a judgment of God.

St. Bridget was recalled to Alvastra by the Prior on account of the illness of her son Benedict, a student there. According to a custom of the time, prevalent in the Benedictine Order also, the boy had assumed the habit when he entered as a pupil; but it was understood that, should he prove to have no vocation, this fact would not oblige him to remain, as he was not under any vows.

However, Benedict desired nothing better than to

[1] Sigtuna is in Sweden, about thirty miles east of Vadstena, and south of Upsala.

persevere in the Order, but he died before he was professed, and his mother closed his eyes.

She remained at Alvastra for some time after his death, though some of the monks were scandalized at her so doing. 'This woman is mad,' said Dom Paul one day. 'Dom Paul is right; I have been mad. He knows me well. I loved the world better than my God; now I desire to serve God only. Go and ask the Prior to pray for me,' said St. Bridget, when she heard Dom Paul's criticism of her conduct.

Her humility disarmed him and all her critics, who recognized that if she was mad, it was the foolishness of the Cross. During her residence at Alvastra she exhorted the monks with great success. Once she told them she had seen in one of her visions that thirty-three of them were about to die soon. Some she saw flying to heaven under the form of doves; others, less perfect, passed through Purgatory first. The first part of this prophecy was fulfilled shortly after, when thirty-three of the monks fell victims to some epidemic, and its realization made a great impression upon the saint's contemporaries.

The Chapters of the Dominican Order were much exercised at this time because so many of the Friars Preachers had been called to be Bishops; the monastery of Sigtuna especially was quite a nursery of prelates. Some of the Fathers did not approve of this, and Blessed Jordan of Saxony and his successors ruled that, for the future, Dominicans should not accept bishoprics unless the Holy Father constrained them to do so in obedience to his will.

The Fathers consulted St. Bridget on this matter,

and she told them that Our Lady had shown her that those who desired the episcopate from worldly motives were not living under the rule of St. Dominic, but those who accepted it from pious motives and reasonable considerations were not excluded from the Order; and if they added the austerity of their Rule to the charge of the episcopate, they merited a double reward. She added that, unfortunately, some of those Friars who became Bishops forgot the cloister and its laws; not because of their work, but because of the honours of their position.

Those who do not accept these Revelations as inspired will agree that the advice they contain was excellent, and certainly showed more than ordinary good sense. It was at this period of the saint's life that the Rule of the Order she was commanded by Our Lord in a vision to found was revealed to her, and this we must reserve for another chapter.

CHAPTER VII

THE RULE AND ORDER OF ST. SAVIOUR

'She hath considered a field and bought it: with the fruit of her hands she hath planted a vineyard.'—PROV. xxxi. 16.

WE now come to the great work of St. Bridget to which the rest of her life was to be devoted—the foundation of the Order of St. Saviour, commonly called the Brigittine Order, one of the most interesting Orders in the Catholic Church. The mother-house of Vadstena, in Sweden, was for over 150 years the centre of Catholicity in that country, and its influence was felt all over Scandinavia. Founded by a princess, who afterwards attained the infinitely higher dignity of a canonized saint of the Church, it attracted as subjects some of the highest nobility of Sweden, even some of royal blood, and some of the most learned men and cultured women of the time. It was the scene of magnificent ecclesiastical functions, attended by Arch-bishops, Bishops, prelates, royal princes, and the principal noblemen of the country, as on the occasion of the translation of the relics of St. Bridget from Rome to Vadstena. It was a place of retreat for Kings and Queens, and was visited by them on several occasions. Its priests—for it was a double monastery of monks and nuns, as we shall explain immediately,

48

—were celebrated all over Sweden as preachers and confessors, and they made many converts to the faith. In fact, we can hardly exaggerate the importance of this monastery, on which no slur was ever cast, though it had some enemies, who tried to damage its reputation. The late King of Sweden, though a Protestant, was intensely interested in it; for being a most accomplished scholar, he knew how great had been its influence in mediæval times, not only in his own country, but in all the north of Europe.

Second to Vadstena, but also of enormous importance, was the once so celebrated Brigittine monastery of Syon House, at Isleworth, in this country. This, too, was an ecclesiastical centre of great force and influence in England in the fifteenth century. King Henry V., in thanksgiving for his victory at Agincourt, founded two royal monasteries on the banks of the Thames—the Carthusian monastery of Sheen and the Brigittine house of Syon—both of which he richly endowed. In 1445, at the suggestion of our English Princess, Queen Philippa of Sweden, daughter of King Richard II., wife of King Eric XIII., a contingent of Brigittine monks and nuns came from Vadstena to found the royal monastery of Syon at Isleworth.

The particular form of spirituality which prevailed at Vadstena suited the English people, and Syon House soon became popular and famous. Subjects from our most noble families joined the community, enriching it with handsome dowries, and for nearly 150 years it enjoyed great prosperity and influence, until Henry VIII., of impious memory, seized its

4

revenues, and expelled its members, who were thus driven into exile.

The Syon House nuns, now at Chudleigh, in Devonshire, enjoy the unique privilege of being the only English pre-Reformation community still existing. In the destruction of so many noble monasteries they alone have survived, after enduring nearly 300 years of exile. They took refuge at Dendermonde in Flanders in 1549; then after a brief return to England under Queen Mary (1553), they were again driven out of their native land, and returned to Belgium, first to Dendermonde, and then to Antwerp. From Antwerp they sought refuge in Rouen, where they stayed fourteen years, and finally found a permanent home in Lisbon, in which hospitable city they were able to enjoy all the privileges of our holy religion unmolested for nearly three centuries. Here they were recruited from time to time from our old Catholic families, until they finally returned to England again in 1861.

They first settled at Spettisbury, in Dorsetshire, where they remained twenty-six years, and in 1887 they moved to their present home at Chudleigh, in Devon. The history of their wanderings is most interesting, but it is not our present purpose to do more than allude to it.

The Brigittine Order in its prime numbered seventy houses. It spread quickly in Sweden, Norway, Denmark, Poland, Germany, France, Bavaria, Holland, and Belgium, and even penetrated into Russia, where it had one monastery at Reval, which was afterwards burnt by schismatics; but most of these convents, except the Polish monasteries, were swept away by the Reformation.

Some fresh ones were opened in the midst of the troubles. Three new ones were founded in Poland, where the greater number of houses was preserved till the middle of the nineteenth century, and a few foundations were made in Flanders and the Netherlands, but these did not last long.

At the present time there exist (exclusive of the Spanish congregations founded by Maria de Escobar, which has five houses in Spain and one in Mexico) only six Brigittine monasteries: one in Bavaria, at Altomunster; two in Holland, at Weert and Uden; two in Mexico; and one in England, at Chudleigh. Altomünster is an ancient foundation, with a most interesting story. We must, however, note that at present there are no longer any Brigittine monks, the double monasteries having been done away with after the Reformation.

In the seventeenth century the French Brigittines lived under a mitigated rule. The nuns appear to have kept schools, and the Fathers adopted the name of Brigittini Novissimi, and established themselves in various places: in France, Flanders, and Germany. The Chapter-General of the Order wanted the Fathers to return to the primitive observance, and when they refused to do so, excluded them from the Order. They eventually died out shortly after from want of means and subjects.

Before we pass to the origin of this great Order, we must not forget to mention the magnificent library, which the monastery of Syon House once possessed. It was one of the finest in England, containing some very valuable manuscripts. It is all dispersed now, but the catalogue is in print, and may be seen at the British Museum.

Vadstena also possessed a very fine library, for among the monks were metaphysicians, astronomers, doctors of canon law, theologians, and literary men; and part of the work of monks and nuns was the transcription of breviaries, prayers, and mystical works of contemporaries, and the copying and illuminating of missals, antiphonaries, and hymnals. They were, indeed, past masters in the art of illumination. When the Order was in its prime, the Brigittine monks supplanted the Benedictines and the Dominicans in Sweden. They occupied the episcopal sees, the most coveted pulpits, and the best professors' chairs in the Universities.

We must now return to St. Bridget, whom we left at Alvastra, where the constitutions of the new Order that Our Lord desired her to found were revealed to her in an ecstasy. She communicated them to the Prior, Father Peter, who translated them into Latin, and wrote them down, without adding or retracting anything from them.

Briefly summarized, they were as follows: Each monastery of the Order of St. Saviour was to be dedicated to the Mother of God, and was to contain both men and women, who were to live in separate wings of the monastery. The church, which was to be common to both communities, was to divide the two convents, and no communication was to be held between the monks and the nuns, except through a grille, through which everything was to be passed from one side to the other.

The choir of the nuns in the church was to be over that of the Fathers, but so arranged that the nuns could see the high altar and the pulpit. Holy Communion was to be given to the nuns through a grille, and none of the monks, except the Confessor-General, was to enter the nuns' quarters, except in the case of the illness of a nun, when her special confessor was admitted to hear her confession.

The Lady Abbess was to hold the same place among the monks that Our Blessed Lady held among the Apostles after Our Lord's Ascension. She was to be supreme in both convents in all temporal matters, and both monks and nuns were to expect everything necessary for their work and welfare from her hands.

In spiritual matters alone the Confessor-General was to have the chief authority, and he was also to be the Prior and rule the monks. The number of monks and nuns in each convent was never to exceed eighty-five — that is, the number of the thirteen Apostles, including St. Paul, and the seventy-two disciples of Our Blessed Lord.

Of these, sixty were to be choir nuns, including the Lady Abbess and the Prioress; thirteen monks were to be priests; two were to be deacons, and two sub-deacons. The priests were to represent the thirteen Apostles, the deacons and sub-deacons the four Doctors of the Church; and there were to be eight choir monks not in Holy Orders.

There were also to be twenty-five lay-brothers,[1] tonsured and cloistered, and some lay-sisters and externs for the domestic labours of the convents, so that the choir members should have plenty of time for prayer and study and the Divine Office.

The novitiate was to last a year, preceded by a year of postulantship ; but in special cases this last might be reduced to six months. No nun could be professed before she was eighteen, and no monk until he was twenty-five. The principal work of the monks was to say or sing Mass, and to act as confessors and chaplains to the nuns. St. Bridget was very clear upon this point, and equally insistent upon the supremacy of the Lady Abbess in temporal matters. Besides ministering to the spiritual needs of the nuns, the Fathers were to preach to and teach the people, and, of course, to recite the Divine Office.

The nuns were to say the Office of Our Lady, according to the Brigittine rite, which is longer than the Divine Office, the lessons which were revealed to the foundress being very long; and the nuns were to say their Hours immediately after the Fathers had finished theirs, so that the *opus magnum* was constantly going on.

The Blessed Sacrament was to be always exposed upon the altar in a ' decent sapphire or crystal vase.' This is one of the most interesting items of the Revelations, because it is one of the earliest records of exposition of the Blessed Sacrament which we

---

[1] Lay brothers and sisters, as we understand the term, were a later institution ; these domestic persons were not religious, or under vows, or members of the Order.

have; and, moreover, there is nothing to lead us to suppose that perpetual adoration was intended, which, indeed, is a later institution. Our Lord's command, as reported by St. Bridget, was 'that the Sacrament of His Body was to be exposed so that they who saw Him under another form daily might desire Him more fervently.'

The nuns were to be strictly enclosed, and only to go outside of the monastery if called to make new foundations. The monks were to leave their convents if the affairs of the Order required them to do so, or if the Bishop of the diocese in which the convent stood needed them, and to convert idolaters and heretics by preaching to them.

Humility was to reign in the monastery, and the poverty was to be absolute. The Rule prescribed sufficient food and baths in order to preserve health. There were to be three days of abstinence a week, and every Friday and Saturday were to be observed as fasts.

Each monastery was to be under the jurisdiction of the Bishop of the diocese in which it stood, and under the protection of the Holy Father. The Bishop was to have the right of visiting the monastery at stated times.

As soon as Father Peter had finished translating the constitutions from Swedish to Latin, they were submitted to Master Matthias and a learned Cistercian Abbot, and then to the Archbishop of Upsala and three of his suffragans, before being sent to Rome for the Papal approbation.

Double monasteries were no innovation; they had

existed in the Church since the days of St. Basil. They were well known in England in the fine old Order of the Gilbertines, founded by St. Gilbert of Sempringham, who died in 1189 at the good old age of 106. He founded a convent first for nuns under the Benedictine Rule, who were most strictly enclosed, and their faces were never to be seen unveiled; the priest was only to have access to them to give them the Sacraments.[1] St. Gilbert then founded some monks whose principal work was to minister to the spiritual needs of the nuns; the monks were to follow the Augustinian Rule. Pope Eugenius III. confirmed the Rule, and St. Gilbert lived to found nine monasteries of his Order.[2] They were entirely suppressed under Henry VIII.

The celebrated Abbey of Whitby, in Yorkshire, is another instance of a double monastery in England. It was founded by St. Hilda (617-680), the grandniece of King Edwin, who was baptized by St. Paulinus. It was said of this saint ' that her prudence was so great that even kings and princes asked and received her advice.'[3]

To the great joy of St. Bridget, Our Lord revealed to her that He desired the first monastery of her Order to be built at Vadstena, a town on the borders of the great Lake Wetter, and on the estate of the saint to whom the suzerainty belonged. Now came the question of funds. St. Bridget had given so much of her own fortune in charity that she had not

[1] *Boll.*, February, vol. i., p. 578.
[2] Heimbucher, 'Orden und Kongregationen,' vol. ii., p. 30.
[3] Bede, 'Eccl. Hist.,' vol. iv., p. 23.

enough left to build and endow a monastery. Her children's fortunes she dared not touch, so she turned to the King and asked Magnus to build a monastery in expiation of his sins.

Magnus had the wit to see that such an institution as Bridget proposed would be as great an advantage to his kingdom as it would be to religion, and granted her request. He and the Queen gave her a royal domain as a site at Vadstena, and also gave a donation of 6,000 silver marks that the first stone might be laid immediately, asking in return that they might be buried in the church of what was destined to be the cradle of the new Order.

CHAPTER VIII

SHE PREACHES REPENTANCE

'Many daughters have gathered together riches: thou hast surpassed them all.'—PROV. xxxi. 29.

By the end of 1346 St. Bridget had finished writing the Rule for her new Order, but she desired once more to visit all her estates and to put her affairs in order before leaving the world; so with the consent of her directors she left what was practically her recluse's cell at Alvastra, and in the company of Father Peter, her chaplain, Father Magnus, and other faithful friends, she set out on a long and arduous journey. The country was mountainous, and the way steep and rough, so as long as the party kept to the road their progress was very slow; but Sweden is plentifully watered with both rivers and lakes, so they wisely made part of the journey by water, embarking on a sailing-boat, and when the wind failed them, they took to the oars.

One evening they disembarked on a little island belonging to St. Bridget, but the inhabitants were asleep, and all their efforts failed to wake them, so the travellers were obliged to pass the cold night without shelter. They shivered on the shore in their

furs, but St. Bridget, who had no furs, but only her
habit of grey homespun, was rapt in ecstasy, and
neither felt nor knew anything of the cold from which
her unfortunate companions were suffering.

Another incident of this trying journey occurred
when they were traversing a virgin forest, infested
with wild animals and robbers. Here the chaplain,
Father Magnus de Motala, was taken dangerously ill,
and fell from his horse in what seems to have been a
fit of some kind. St. Bridget healed him by placing
her hands on his head, and then made him remount.
Further on, when they reached the shore of Lake
Wetter, they were stopped by one of St. Bridget's
vassals, who complained to her that he could not
marry his daughter for want of a dowry, whereupon
St. Bridget commanded her steward to give him all
the money they had with them. He demurred at
this, but apparently from unworthy motives, for he
turned out to be untrustworthy. But the saint insisted upon her wishes being obeyed.

'I belong to these poor people,' she said; 'they
have only me to look to in their poverty. I abandon
myself to the Divine will.'

Idolatry had only just given place to Christianity
in some of the districts they passed through, and by
the advice of St. Bridget, Father Peter of Alvastra
preached to the people, and reconciled them to the
Church,[1] they promising to keep the faith. During
these travels, which appear to have lasted some
weeks, St. Bridget is said to have healed numerous
epileptics, and people who in those days were said to

[1] Flavigny, p. 158.

be possessed with devils, but most of whom we should probably call insane.

Before returning to Alvastra, St. Bridget went to Skara, and then to Lincoping, to see her director, Master Matthias, who, during her stay, publicly defended her Revelations in the pulpit from an attack which had been made upon them by a certain monk, and at the same time he praised her very highly also.

Her humility made her remonstrate with Master Matthias afterwards, saying she needed his prayers, for this was only the beginning of her life, and that it would be better to wait until the end to see if she was worthy of the praise he had bestowed upon her.

Vadstena is not more than twelve miles from Alvastra, both of which places are on the eastern side of the great Lake Wetter, on the shores of which the new monastery was to be built. On an ancient historical map of Sweden may be seen a smaller lake between these two towns, with a river connecting it with Lake Wetter.

After her return to her cell at Alvastra, St. Bridget constantly visited the site of the new monastery, which now filled so much of her mind, and was so near to her heart. She appears to have made these journeys to and fro upon horseback, and on one occasion, when she was going in all probability to lay the foundation-stone, she fell into an ecstasy while riding, and when they reached the Cistercian monastery near Vadstena was still rapt in it. Here refreshments were provided for the tired travellers, and one of her companions, most likely the Prior, Father Peter, roused the saint from her rapture to partake of a meal, and was reproached by her for so doing.

During some of these journeys to and from Vadstena, St. Bridget is said to have walked across the little lake mentioned above, to the amazement and admiration of the bystanders, who frequently witnessed the miracle.

She was now to be taken from her beloved seclusion at Alvastra, for Our Lord had other work for her to do. At this time Pope Clement VI., following the precedent of his three predecessors, was residing at Avignon, and St. Bridget, who was well versed in all contemporary events, knew what disastrous results the exile of the papacy had had upon the Catholic world; for at Avignon the Pope was to some extent a dependent of the King of France, and the authority of the Holy See was no longer respected as it ought to have been. Moreover, in consequence of the diminution of the Pope's influence, Europe was disturbed with wars and struggles of various kinds.

Edward III. of England was disputing the throne of France with Philip of Valois, and had already gained the great victory of Crecy, which had plunged all France into grief, while war was still raging between the two Kings. St. Bridget now wrote a most remarkable letter to Clement VI., in which she urged him in the strongest terms to make peace between the Kings of England and France, and to go himself to Rome, and there to celebrate the jubilee year. She spoke, or rather wrote, to the Pope in the name of Our Lord, who, she said, had revealed to her all these things. She rebuked Clement most severely for his past negli-

gence, and warned him that God would speedily call
him to his account unless he obeyed these injunctions,
and all this was set forth in the plainest and most
forcible language.   Never before or since was such a
letter penned by a dutiful subject to a Pope, except,
perhaps, by St. Catherine of Siena to Urban VI., as
this of St. Bridget's to Clement VI.   Philip-le-Bel's
historic quarrel with Boniface VIII., which drew from
that Pope the celebrated Bull, ' Clericis Laicos,' as-
serting that the laity had always been hostile to the
clergy, certainly elicited a most sarcastic letter from
Philip to Boniface VIII., in which the King claimed
the right to levy taxes on the clergy, but then Philip-
le-Bel could not be described as a dutiful subject.   St.
Bridget sent her letter to Avignon by Father Peter of
Alvastra and Hemming, Bishop of Abo, and the Pope
received it with both respect and deference, and sent
the Bishop at once to restore peace between Edward III.
and Philip IV.

Hemming failed in this mission, and St. Bridget
was on this occasion gifted with the power of biloca-
tion, or being in two places at the same time—a
power in which Oriental mystics of the present day
believe quite as firmly as mediæval Christians did.
This holy Bishop of Abo firmly believed that St.
Bridget, who was certainly at that time in Sweden, appeared to him in France, and encouraged him to obey
the Pope in every detail, and comforted him for his
failure in the difficult task set him.

At this time Magnus II. desired his cousin St.
Bridget to come to his Court, and Father Peter
ordered her to obey the summons, and as she

believed it to be the will of God that she should go, she went.

Magnus, who was still in great financial difficulties, was contemplating an expedition against the pagans of Livonia and Ethonia, hoping to enrich himself by despoiling the Russians, and had sent for St. Bridget to ask for her prayers for success, not for her advice on the subject, which he nevertheless received. St. Bridget, seeing through his motives, discouraged him from the undertaking, urging him not to incur further expenses, and offering her two sons, Charles and Birger, as hostages to his creditors till he was able to discharge his debts; but although these young noblemen were rich, their fortunes would have been but a drop in the ocean of the King's debts, so he refused the offer.

St. Bridget's sojourn at the Court this time was fraught with ridicule, abuse, and actual insult. Her solemn warnings to the Kings, Queens, and courtiers only brought her contempt and petty persecution; the young princes, including her godson Eric, mocked her and jeered at her, but she did not on this account hesitate to rebuke them all in the severest terms for their worldliness and vices. On one occasion a nephew of the holy Bishop Brynolf, who pretended to think that she had injured him at Court, poured a quantity of iced water over her as she passed under his windows; but she only shook her homespun habit, and thanked God gaily for sending her such a mortification, as she passed on to the cathedral.

At the end of 1349 Clement VI. announced a jubilee for the following year in a Bull calling all the faithful to Rome. St. Bridget was troubled at the invitation, which she thought she ought to accept, since at present she was not needed in Sweden, where she had failed in her mission to the Court, and she also felt herself at this time powerless to found the new monastery at Vadstena; yet she hesitated to leave her children, who she feared would fall a prey to the vices of the Court unless she were near them to control them.

CHAPTER IX

DEPARTURE FOR ROME

'Strength and beauty are her clothing, and she shall laugh in the latter day.'—PROV. xxxi. 25.

IT may be a sad thought, but it is certainly a true one, that the natural affections of the saints endear them more to us than their supernatural virtues, which seem to raise them so far above us. So St. Bridget attracts us more at this particular time of her life, when her human affections cause her to hesitate to obey the call to Rome, than when she is rapt in ecstasy, or preaching repentance, or prophesying, or reforming the clergy and religious Orders, or labouring to bring the Pope back to Rome, or dictating her Revelations.

To understand why she hesitated to go to Rome, we must pause a moment to see what claims her family, who were no longer children, had upon her. Her eldest daughter, Martha, who, it will be remembered, had made a marriage her mother rightly disapproved of, had lost her first husband, Sigfried Ribbing, after living very unhappily with him, and had married again. Her second husband, Canute Algotson, was as rich and powerful as Sigfried had been, and Martha was living a very worldly life of great luxury at Court, which distressed her mother, who reproached herself bitterly for having brought up her children in splendour, and taught them to live according to their high rank.

Her eldest son, Charles, now Seneschal of Nericia and a knight, instead of fulfilling the duties of his station, contented himself with leading an idle life at the Court of Magnus. He, too, had been twice married. His second wife was a beautiful Norwegian Princess named Gisla; but Charles was not a faithful husband, and spent his time in sharing the voluptuous pleasures of the King and Court. He was a very violent, passionate man, but he was also a firm believer in the truths of religion, and had a great devotion to Our Lady. His mother had immense influence over him, and frequently brought him to repentance; but he soon forgot all his good resolutions and promises of amendment, and lapsed again into sin. Ulf had always spoilt his eldest son, and neglected to correct his faults, while taking delight in his manly qualities; consequently Charles had been a constant trial and source of anxiety to his saintly mother, who never ceased to pray for him.

Birger, her second son, was very different. He never caused his mother any trouble by bad conduct; all her fears for him were lest the gay and corrupt Court at Stockholm should lead him astray. He was very austere, and his manner of life made him very lonely, for naturally it did not attract the frivolous, worldly courtiers by whom he was surrounded. His mother was his confidante, and St. Bridget feared, if she went to Rome and left him, he would have no one

to turn to for sympathy in the battle of life. All
these considerations, then, made her shrink from
going so far from her family.

Of her other children, Benedict and Gudmar were
already dead. Ingeborg was a nun, and Cecilia, her
youngest child, had entered the Dominican convent
at Skening by her mother's wish, but against her own
inclination, as a novice; and it seemed probable that
she had no vocation, and would have to leave, and in
that case would need her mother at hand to receive
her. It eventually turned out that Cecilia really had
no vocation for the religious life, for she left Skening,
and was twice married, the first time to a great friend
of her brother Charles, an officer of high rank. There
remained one other child, Catherine, St. Bridget's
second daughter and future life companion, and co-
foundress of the Order of St. Saviour, details of whose
career we must reserve for a separate chapter, for she
henceforth played a very important part in the history
of the Order which her mother was about to found,
and was also an indefatigable worker for her mother's
canonization.

While St. Bridget was thus hesitating, and very
unhappy as to her future plans, she had a vision in
which Our Lord showed her that He wished her to go
to Rome, and trust her children to Him, and Our
Lady herself promised to be a mother to them. St.
Bridget at once obeyed, and told Father Peter of
Skening, her confessor, her resolution, and begged
- him to get ready to accompany her.

She left Sweden, according to the best authorities,
in 1349, accompanied by Father Peter of Skening, who

was her faithful companion in all her pilgrimages, her confessor, guide, and ruler of her house in Rome for thirty years; her stewards and almoners; Father Magnus de Motala and Gudmar; an old friend, Ingeborg, the unhappy wife of one Nicholas Danaes; and a few servants; but by none of her children. Some writers, say that the Prior of Alvastra also accompanied her on this journey, others do not mention him; but he certainly joined her in Rome later on. The similarity of his name and the other Father Peter Olafson of Skening has led to confusion among some of her biographers.

The plague was raging on the Continent at this time, and perhaps for this reason St. Bridget's party did not follow the usual route of pilgrims to the Eternal City. They embarked at Stralsund, the people weeping to see St. Bridget leave her native country, and crying that the guardian angel of the kingdom was flying from them and abandoning them to the Divine wrath. The pilgrims then took the route St. Bridget had followed with Ulf on their first visit to Rome. This revived her grief at his loss, and she felt the need of human sympathy. Then it was that Our Lord promised her a friend and companion in her exile, who should share in all her sufferings and labours, and in her spiritual joys; but he did not mention St. Catherine's name. It was not until her daughter joined her a few years later that St. Bridget recognized the fulfilment of this promise.

The travellers sometimes rode on horseback, sometimes walked, and were entertained in castles and

convents, St. Bridget trying to conceal her rank, but
often revealing it by her generosity. They stopped at
Milan to venerate the relics of St. Ambrose, who
appeared to our saint, and encouraged her in her
work, and sent a message by her to the Archbishop,
which she delivered, though he declined to pay much
attention to it. Just as they were on the point of
leaving Milan, St. Bridget's friend, Ingeborg Danaes,
was taken very ill and died, and after burying her,
the pilgrims resumed their journey to Pavia and
Genoa. At Genoa they were again detained by the
illness of one of the party, and St. Bridget passed her
days and often her nights in prayer and ecstasy
before a celebrated picture of the Crucifixion in a
hermitage at Quarto, a village near Genoa, where
the pilgrims lodged in some cottages adjoining this
hermitage.

It is believed that they took a boat at Genoa for
Ostia, for any records of their journey by land from
Genoa to Rome are lost. Numbers of pilgrims, of all
nations and all classes, were going to Rome for the
Jubilee, some on horseback, some on foot, all in
danger from the Black Death or plague.

When they arrived in sight of Rome St. Bridget
fell upon her knees and cried with the other pilgrims,
' Sancte Petre, Sancte Paule, misericordia.'[1] When at
last St. Bridget entered the Church of St. Peter, the
crowd was so great that she had to wait for hours
before she could approach near to offer her homage
and prayers at the tomb of St. Peter.

We may gather some idea of the state of Rome at

---

[1] Flavigny, 'La Vie de Ste. Brigitte,' p. 235.

this time from Muratori.[1] He tells us that Rome
without the Pope had become almost a wilderness.
'Brute force had taken the place of justice; there
was no observance of the laws, no protection of
property, no personal safety. The pilgrims who came
to visit the tombs of the Apostles were plundered, the
peasants attacked at the very gates of the city; women
and girls were outraged; the churches were falling to
pieces; cattle were grazing in St. Peter's and the
Lateran; the Forum had become a kitchen-garden
and a resting-place for animals. One consequence of
the removal of the Papal Chair was internal dissen-
sion; the population was decreasing, and the people
becoming uncivilized.' To add to all this terrible
state of affairs, in Rome itself the Black Death was
carrying off half the population of Italy.

Rienzi, the Roman patriot, who had risen to the
position of dictator, and had lately been deposed from
it, was now a prisoner in a dungeon at Avignon; but
the struggle was still raging between the nobles and
the people, and St. Bridget, whose sympathies were
all with her own class, thought he was justly treated.
We may not linger here over the romantic and oft-
told story of Rienzi. He was liberated by Clement's
successor, Pope Innocent VI., who sent him back to
Rome to crush the power and tyranny of the nobles.
This he did successfully, but he became so unpopular
by his haughtiness that he was murdered by the
Roman citizens.

A bitter disappointment awaited St. Bridget on
her arrival in Rome. The Pope, Clement VI., had

---

[1] Muratori, 'Fragmenta Historiæ Romanæ,' tom. iii.

paid no attention to her letter entreating him to return to his see, and was still at Avignon, in the magnificent papal palace there, and the saint at once realized that the great work Our Lord intended her to do in the centre of Christendom was to induce the Pope to return to his capital, whither his duty and the needs of the Church called him.

The principal note of this Jubilee which Clement had proclaimed was penance. It was called the Jubilee of Remission, and on Christmas Eve, which fell soon after St. Bridget arrived, crowds of pilgrims visited the four basilicas within the walls of the city, while she prayed at St. Peter's for the return of the Pope, and for the priests and people of Rome, who so sorely needed her prayers. Here she had a vision in which she saw Our Lady, and heard a voice cry, ' Oh, Rome! Rome! thy walls are destroyed, thy gates broken, thy altars desolate; the living sacrifice and the morning offering are banished from thy courts; the sweet incense no longer goes up from thy holy places.'

A great argument in favour of the truth of the Revelations of St. Bridget is that they always prompted her to good works, and on coming out of this ecstasy she at once set to work to help and succour the pilgrims, with whom the city was crowded, and exhort them to repentance; to tend the sick, and by her example excite the rich to imitate her. She made the Swedish pilgrims her special charge, and all of her country men and women who were in need of hospitality found it under her roof, where she personally attended to them. She nursed the sick, and frequently healed them by supernatural means. She mended the clothing of the poor, and accompanied those who went round the city to beg for food or alms from the monasteries. Her house was most plainly furnished, and the refreshment offered to the pilgrims was of the most frugal kind, for already she was practising the poverty which was to be one of the notes of her Order. She began to live by rule as soon as she settled in Rome. She rose at four every morning, and after she had been to confession, heard Mass, and then went to St. Peter's, or one of the other basilicas, to assist at whatever service might be proceeding; and about nine o'clock the Swedish pilgrims took their repast in the refectory, where she presided, saying prayers before and after the meal aloud. From then till Vespers she divided her time between prayer and manual labour, for although Father Peter, who arranged every detail of her household, obliged her to keep a great many servants, she delighted in performing the most humble offices. In the evening she went to church for Vespers and Compline; after supper there was a short recreation, and when the others retired at eight o'clock the saint began her vigil. Thus she inaugurated her work in Rome.

CHAPTER X

CATHERINE OF SWEDEN

'Honour widows that are widows indeed.'—1 TIM. v. 3.

ST. BRIDGET's second daughter, Catherine, was also a
canonized saint of the Church, though for many years
the Bull of her canonization was lost. She was a
most lovable creature, very beautiful, and most sweet
and amiable, and her very weaknesses endear her to
us, for she was in some ways very human, and cast in
a softer mould than her more celebrated mother. In
personal appearance they were a great contrast, for
St. Bridget was very small and fair, and Catherine
was a tall, fine woman, of exceptional beauty, which
caused her a great deal of trouble and inconvenience
in those rough times when enclosure was often necessary to protect nuns from the violence of men.

As a little child Catherine used to accompany her
mother in her visits to the sick poor and to the
hospitals, and St. Bridget's friends sometimes remonstrated with her for taking so young a child to see
such sad sights; but she only answered that it taught
her little daughter to love the sufferers, and in St.
Catherine's case the experiment certainly answered,
as we shall see.

When she was between fourteen and fifteen,

Catherine, in obedience to her father, Ulf, but contrary to her own wishes, inasmuch as she desired to consecrate her life entirely to Almighty God, consented to marry a very devout young nobleman named Egard, and with him she lived a life of angelical purity and great austerity. They slept on the floor, and even in the cold of a Swedish winter never allowed themselves a mattress nor more than one blanket and a pillow apiece. They often rose, not only for Matins, but also for vigils spent in prayers and genuflections. Shortly after her marriage Catherine adopted the antique costume of the country, which the nobility had discarded in favour of more modern fashions, and no mockery, such as that in which her brother Charles indulged, could make her change. Many other ladies, friends of Catherine's, followed her example, and also left off wearing superfluous ornaments. Her sister-in-law, Gisla, Charles's wife, first resisted, and then copied Catherine, much to her husband's wrath, who told his sister she not only made herself a nun, but, not content with that, she made one of his wife also.

Catherine is usually represented with a stag nestling up to her, because one day when Egard was out stag-hunting, with hounds and men on horseback, she happened to drive past, and the hunted deer jumped into the carriage in its terror and took shelter under her cloak. When Egard and the other hunters rode up and demanded the stag, we are told that Catherine very humbly begged her husband to spare its life, and he granted her request.

Her father Ulf died soon after her marriage, and when St. Bridget went to Rome, Catherine soon began to have a great longing to make a pilgrimage there. Egard, seeing she was troubled about something, asked her what was the matter, and she told him; but he, fearing that so young and beautiful a woman would be in danger if she undertook so long a journey alone, hesitated to consent, but finally, conquered by her entreaties and prayers, he yielded. Her brother Charles, however, happening to hear of it, wrote to Egard, with characteristic violence threatening to kill him if he dared to allow his sister to make a pilgrimage out of her own country. This letter fell into Catherine's hands, and she sent it to her Uncle Israel, St. Bridget's brother, a very pious man of great influence. He told her not to be induced by Charles's threats to abandon her holy proposal, and, promising to ward off his anger from Egard, counselled her to start without delay. She at once set sail with the Marshal of Sweden and two other ladies, and after a difficult voyage, they travelled through Germany and Italy and reached Rome in August.

St. Bridget was absent at the time of their arrival. She had gone to Bologna to correct and admonish the Superior of a religious house at Farfa, and Father Peter Olaf and a few other members of her household were with her. For eight days Catherine sought her mother with great anxiety, and then Father Peter in Bologna was seized with a great desire to return to Rome. He could neither eat nor sleep, and St. Bridget very unwillingly let him return. There he met Catherine and her companions in St. Peter's, and received her with great joy, understanding now why he had felt impelled to return to the city. The next day

they all went to Farfa[1] to see St. Bridget, and were
reverently received by the Abbot, and stayed some
days there, and then returned to Rome and fulfilled
the pilgrimage to the tombs of the Apostles and the
churches of the stations.

After St. Catherine had been some weeks in Rome
she wished to go home to Egard, but St. Bridget,
who was now convinced that this was the companion
Our Lord had promised to send her, begged her
daughter for the love of Him to remain, since it had
been revealed to her that Catherine's husband would
have passed from this world before she could reach
their home in Sweden. Catherine consented to stay
with her mother, in whose revelations she had firm
faith ; but the human and most natural longing to
return to Egard constantly recurred, and St. Bridget
and Father Peter had to use all their influence to
induce her to overcome it. Her biographer gives us a
very natural picture of a subsequent attack of home-
sickness on St. Catherine's part, which, as it shows
her character and also the kind of trial to which her
sojourn in Rome subjected her, we must relate. As
we know, Rome was in a most unsettled state, and
was infested with ruffians, who made it unsafe for the
pilgrims to make the stations ; so St. Bridget forbade
Catherine to go out, or to visit the holy places, unless
she had a powerful escort, which apparently was not

[1] Old writers call this place Sarpa ; Papebrochius calls it
Parpa ; but the learned writer in the 'Acta Sanctorum' says it
was properly Farfa, because there was a celebrated monastery
of that name in Italy in the time of St. Bridget. See *Boll.*,
October, vol. iv., p. 460.

always forthcoming. So the poor child—she was only eighteen—was left at home for several days, while St. Bridget and Father Peter were visiting the indulgenced churches. It is not to be wondered at under these trying circumstances, away from her husband and all her friends, and also cut off from the spiritual privileges of Rome, that she became very unhappy and depressed; and when the others returned one day, they found her pale as death, and weeping so bitterly that she could not speak. That night she had a vision, in which Our Lady appeared to her, and the saint implored her help. Our Lady told her to be obedient to her mother and confessor, and to remain in Rome.

She rose immediately and went to Bridget, and, falling on her knees, begged her to forgive her for her disobedience, and told her of her vision, and promised to be resigned to remaining in exile with her until death. Wishing to test her daughter's humility, St. Bridget sent for Father Peter, and Catherine made a promise of obedience to him, and faithfully kept it. Nor must we imagine that in this St. Bridget exacted more of her daughter than she practised herself, for though to her naturally imperious temperament obedience to another was very difficult, yet she herself obeyed Father Peter implicitly in every detail. He controlled her household, and governed her temporal as well as her spiritual affairs; and if ever she was wanting in obedience, she begged his pardon on her knees most humbly, and submitted herself so entirely to him that she did not even raise her eyes from the ground without his permission, and the more painful the command he gave her, the more prompt was she to obey. She learnt some Latin from him in Rome, although she knew he was not a good classical scholar. After the death of her director, Father Matthias, which was revealed to her not many years after her arrival in Rome, she had to lean more upon Father Peter.

But we must return to St. Catherine, who became a widow two years after her arrival in Rome. She lived in her mother's house, near the Campo dei Fiori, with Father Peter as her director and teacher of the Rule of St. Saviour. Here she learnt to keep silence at certain times in the day, to help and comfort the pilgrims and the poor with alms and familiar conversation, exhorting them to patience and the love of Our Lord. One pilgrim, whom she frequently instructed, went with her when at last, after her mother's death, she returned to Sweden, and became a lay-brother at Vadstena.

After Catherine was left a widow she had many suitors, for her beauty was extraordinary, and many Roman nobles desired to marry her, and promised her a large marriage settlement if she would accept them. She refused them all, telling them she was under a vow of perpetual chastity. Some of them were so much in love with her that more than once they lay in wait for her, as she went to church, to carry her off by force. A beautiful little story is told of her in this connection. We have heard how one day she saved the life of a stag; now on this occasion a stag saved her. She was going one day to visit the Church of St. Sebastian Fuori-le-Mura with some noble Roman matrons, when a certain count, who was in love with her, and was one of her rejected suitors, lay in wait

with a large escort of armed men to carry her off.
Just as they hastened from their hiding-place to seize
her a stag started out from a thicket, and they were
so occupied in hunting it that Catherine and her
friends made good their escape to Rome.

From that day Catherine did not dare to go openly
to the stations, or to venture outside the city, unless
St. Bridget had been forewarned in prayer that it
would be safe for her to go. Nevertheless, on two
other occasions Catherine was very nearly captured,
and only escaped by a miracle.

She rivalled her mother in austerities. She always
passed four hours before going to rest at night in
genuflections, beating her breast, and meditating on
the Passion with many tears. After a short night's
rest she rose again before dawn to pray, and unless
called away did not cease her devotions till noon.

One little legend of this fascinating saint we must
record, and then return to St. Bridget, in whose
history Catherine's became merged during the rest of
the elder saint's life.

Catherine was walking outside Rome one day with
some Roman ladies, when they noticed some grapes
hanging over the wall of a vineyard which they were
passing, and as Catherine was the tallest of the party,
they asked her to gather some for them. She had on
a dress with torn sleeves, frayed and worn, because of
the poverty she had chosen; but as she reached up
her arm to gather the grapes, the sleeves appeared
to the others to be of purple and gold and of some
precious material, and they in amazement touched
them (we can see them doing it), and said: 'Oh,

Lady Catherine! who would ever believe you would wear such costly clothing?' The servants and Father Peter, who knew how old a dress Catherine had on, heard this remark, and drew their own conclusion, shared by Catherine's biographer, that it was preternatural. At any rate, it is a pretty story, and no doubt Catherine's rags were much more precious in the eyes of Our Lord, for whose dear sake they were worn, than the most precious clothing would have been.

This was the companion Our Lord had given His spouse in the work He had called her to do, and she must have been a great comfort to St. Bridget, for she was as amiable as she was beautiful, and one of her nieces, who lived with her for five years at Vadstena, records that she never heard a word of anger or impatience from her.

CHAPTER XI

LIFE AND WORK IN ROME

'She hath put her hand to strong things, and her fingers have taken hold of the spindle.'—PROV. xxxi. 19.

THE Farfa monastery, at which the meeting between St. Bridget and St. Catherine took place, was a magnificent building, but the discipline was terribly relaxed, and the Abbot was a very worldly man. On the arrival of St. Bridget, whose fame had reached him, he refused to admit her and her party inside the monastery, on the ground that it was contrary to the holy Rule to permit women to enter it, and he gave her a lodging in a place inferior to that in which he kept his dogs and falcons.

Nothing daunted by this treatment, the Swedish Princess and former mistress of the royal palace at Stockholm insisted upon seeing him, and during her stay had several interviews with him, and remonstrated with him upon his conduct as Abbot, and upon the luxury he permitted himself and his monks, threatening him with the visitation of God if he did not reform.

Some writers say that he listened to the saint, but in the third book of the Revelations we read that 'he was a very worldly man, who troubled himself nothing about souls, and that he died suddenly without the Sacraments.'[1]

If Father Peter, the Prior of Alvastra, did not travel to Rome with St. Bridget, he joined her there soon after, and remained with her for some time, acting as one of her confessors and directors for the rest of her life. Another of her counsellors, who exercised a great influence over her after he made her acquaintance in 1352, was Alphonsus of Vadaterra, the holy Bishop of Jaen, whose father was a Sienese, and whose mother an Italian. It is said that he stood in nearer relations with St. Bridget, both as a friend and as spiritual Father, than either of her Swedish confessors. He gave up his bishopric to go to Rome, and lived in retreat as an Augustinian hermit. He had the greatest admiration and regard for St. Bridget, who consulted him about her Rule and Constitutions. Later he defended the Revelations, in whose genuineness he firmly believed, and wrote an introduction to them.

Our Lord never left the saint without counsellors and directors, to whom she communicated her mystical experiences, and whom she consulted in all her various works.

Just before St. Catherine reached Rome the Cardinal Legate and Vicar, Annibaldo de Ceccano, had excommunicated Cola di Rienzi, and laid the city under an interdict for eight days, according to the Comtesse de Flavigny.[2] He was very unpopular, and had already punished the people by abridging the

---

[1] 'Revelationes,' Lib. III.

[2] Flavigny, 'Vie de Ste. Brigitte.'

Jubilee, and in revenge they had attempted his life by shooting at him with an arrow, which pierced the brim of his hat, as he was entering the basilica of St. Paul's. The interdict he then proclaimed was removed by the time St. Bridget and St. Catherine returned from Bologna, and took up their residence in the house[1] Cardinal Hugh Roger, brother of Clement VI., whose title was of San Lorenzo in Damaso, had let to her, which was near the church of that name.

By the time the Swedish seer had been a year in Rome she exercised a great influence on all classes of society, from the poorest pilgrims to the highest nobility. She converted many sinners, directed many energetic, virtuous persons, and made many disciples; but it was Catherine who comforted the broken-hearted and consoled the miserable. She could speak Italian, and knew Latin well, and used to receive in her cell the ignorant to teach, the weak to strengthen, the wounded in heart, or soul, or body to heal, the dead in sin to revive. The beautiful young widow was powerful to help where the mystic was powerless. St. Catherine sought the lost sheep, the feeble, wounded lambs; while St. Bridget attracted as her followers strong, healthy, or already healed souls, ' brave to suffer,' capable of endurance. One saint was the complement of the other, each worked in her own sphere, and between them all sorts and conditions of men were influenced for good. Catherine's own

---

[1] This house, which St. Bridget lived in for years, belonged to Cardinal Hugh Roger from 1342-1363, but he lived at Avignon or elsewhere in France. See *Boll.*, October, vol. iv., p. 461.

sorrows had taught her to feel for others, for when the news of Egard's death reached her, we are told that she nearly died of grief, and only her faith prevented her from attempting self-destruction; and after her recovery her mother's prayers alone enabled her to settle down to her life in Rome, to which she was supernaturally called, but which she felt to be exile from her country and her friends. Her beauty was such a source of annoyance to her, curtailing her freedom as it did, since her admirers constantly attempted to carry her off by force, that she determined to destroy it. She mixed some poisons with a lotion, intending to anoint her face with it and spoil her beautiful complexion. Father Peter Olafson and her mother, on hearing of her intention, forbade her to do so; but Catherine made no answer to their remonstrances, and went to a lonely grotto, where no one could interrupt her, to carry out her design. Just as she was on the point of applying the poisonous mixture to her face a large stone fell from the roof of the grotto, breaking the bottle and knocking her to the ground. Her forehead was cut open, and she bore the scar for the rest of her life; but she now recognized that the sacrifice she had proposed to make was not acceptable to Almighty God, and desisted from any further attempt.

While the two saints were living this life of religious retirement, St. Catherine teaching and consoling the ignorant and miserable and St. Bridget preaching, the struggle between the nobility and the Roman people was still going on, and the din of the civil war between the two parties penetrated to the oratory of St.

Bridget's house. The two great noble Roman families of Orsini and Colonna, whose rivalry had formerly been the cause of much bloodshed, had recently been reconciled, probably by St. Bridget's means, and they now united to seize the reins of government; but for some reason Pope Clement VI. did not approve of this, annulled the election of the two Counts, and banished them, much to the surprise of the two Swedish saints. A state of anarchy in Rome was the result.

At this juncture St. Bridget told her confessors and the Cardinals Orsini and de Grimondo, her friends, that she had had a vision, in which Our Lord had said to her: 'Remain in Rome until you shall see the Pope and the Emperor there. You will then tell them in My Name the words with which I shall inspire you.'[1] The astonishment of the Cardinals and confessors was so great at this communication that they could hardly believe it, and they asked the saint if she had forgotten that the Pope and the Emperor had been at variance for years. Did she not remember that the Popes John XXII. and Benedict XII. had refused to recognize Louis of Bavaria, who had been irregularly elected to the Empire, and the struggle which had ensued thereupon? Had she forgotten that the German Sovereign had dared to instal an Antipope in the Vatican, and that although now the Antipope had submitted, and Charles, King of Bohemia, had (in 1347) been chosen Emperor, with the consent of the Holy See, and Charles had promised to enter Rome, only to receive the imperial crown

[1] 'Revelationes Extravagantes,' Lib. VIII.

from the Pope, and Clement VI. had not the remotest
intention of crowning him in the Eternal City?

St. Bridget listened to all these questions, but she
never doubted Our Lord would keep His promise to
her, in spite of the apparent impossibility of its fulfilment, and, as it turned out, the death of Clement VI.,
in 1352, prepared the way for this.

On December the 2nd in that year the bells of St.
Peter's were struck by lightning and melted, and the
people declared that it presaged the death of the Pope,
who was then dangerously ill at Avignon. St. Bridget
at once set herself to pray earnestly for the Pope's
soul, and he died fortified by the Sacraments of the
Church.

Clement had many very good qualities. He was a
Benedictine monk, and he faithfully fulfilled his
monastic duties.[1] He was very charitable, and
charity, as we know, 'covers a multitude of sins.'
During the time of the plague which raged at
Avignon he refused to leave the city, and showed
great zeal, courage, and love for the sufferers. He
paid for doctors and nurses to attend the poor, bought
for them the necessaries of life, gave large sums of
money for the transport and burial of the dead, and
took all the then known precautions for preventing
the spread of the disease.[2] On the other hand, he
was very extravagant in lavishing benefits on his own
family, and weak in correcting his friends. He encouraged his courtiers in luxury, and, as Our Lord
told St. Bridget, thought more of the bodies than the
souls of the people under his care. He had many

[1] Flavigny, p. 285.   [2] *Ibid.*

enemies who belittled his memory, as well as many friends among the French, who were his countrymen, and who exalted his virtues.

The Conclave which sat after his death elected Cardinal Stephen d'Albert as his successor, who took the title of Innocent VI. Our Lord revealed to St. Bridget at the time of this Pope's enthronement that he would soon be taken from the world through the malice of men. Almost immediately after his election fresh discord, augmented by a famine, broke out in Rome, and Orsini was killed in a riot near the Campo dei Fiori. The people knew that he was a friend of St. Bridget, and when she, attracted by the noise, came to the window, they called her witch and sorceress, and even talked of burning her alive. Calm was at length restored by the Cardinal Legate Albornoz, whom the new Pope had appointed. Albornoz was now at Montefiascone, the only town in Italy which had remained faithful to Innocent, and he now took the step of liberating Cola de Rienzi, and sending him back to Rome to govern the city.

Soon after the return of Rienzi the secretary of Cardinal Hugh Roger wrote to St. Bridget, and informed her that His Eminence could no longer let her have the house near St. Laurence in Damaso, in which she was living, but he allowed her one month to look for another.

This was not an easy task for two foreigners, who were known to be poor, and were by no means popular with the citizens, and the saint wandered about Rome, for this month of grace searching for somewhere to live, but without success. The people refused to let

her a suitable house. In her distress, which seems
to have been very great, she turned to Our Lord, as
she was wont to do in all her troubles; and at the
last moment, when the month had just expired, He
heard her, and revealed to her that He had suffered
this trial to befall her to try her, and soon there came
a letter from Cardinal Hugh Roger from Avignon
authorizing her to remain in his house as long as she
liked. Not long after a rich Roman lady, Francesca
de Papazurri, who had a palace near the Campo dei
Fiori, with beautiful orange gardens, gave it to St.
Bridget, and she and Catherine moved into it; but
here fresh troubles awaited them.

CHAPTER XII

TROUBLES AND TRIALS IN ROME

'She hath looked well to the paths of her house, and hath not
eaten her bread in idleness.'—PROV. xxxi. 27.

THE house St. Bridget's friend and disciple, Francesca
de Papazurri, gave her is still called St. Bridget's
house, and is now inhabited by a community of nuns.
In giving this house Francesca gave all she had to
spare, and as the funds which Bridget and Catherine
had brought from Sweden were now exhausted, and
there was much difficulty in getting their income from
their own country, they now found themselves unable
to furnish their new house properly, or to keep up the
gardens. Indeed, they could scarcely afford to buy
the necessary food for their household, and St. Bridget
sometimes went with the beggars to the gate of the
Poor Clares at St. Laurence in Panisperna to beg for
bread. But this did not suffice for her family, so,
after consulting Our Lord, she was obliged to borrow
money. He told her to undertake to pay it back on
the Octave of the Epiphany, and with her usual trust
in His Providence she promised, though at the time,
humanly speaking, there seemed little chance of her
being able to do so. On the very day, however, a

messenger arrived from Sweden with remittances which enabled the saint to pay her debts.

Later on, the Swedish Princess was again obliged to borrow money, and this time she fixed upon Whitsuntide to discharge her debt, and on that day one of her Swedish debtors arrived with gold and silver for her, and again she was able to fulfil her promise.

Another time Catherine was assisting at Mass in St. Peter's, and prayed to Our Father to give them their daily bread; as she did so a Dominican tertiary, wearing the Dominican habit, as was the custom for tertiaries in those days, came up to her, and said: 'Dear lady, pray for Gisla.' Gisla, it will be remembered, was her sister-in-law, Charles's wife, the Seneschal of Nericia.

'Where do you come from?' said Catherine. The stranger replied that she came from Sweden to tell her countrymen of the premature death of the Seneschal's wife.

Catherine begged her to go home with her and see her mother, but the unknown pilgrim refused, saying that God would speedily deliver Catherine and St. Bridget from the poverty from which they were now suffering, and that shortly a golden crown, which Gisla had left Catherine in her will, would be brought to her by a messenger. The mysterious stranger then disappeared, and Catherine asked her attendants, one of whom was Father Peter, if they had seen the tertiary to whom she had been speaking; but they replied that they had seen no one, though they had heard her conversing with someone. On Catherine's return to her home St. Bridget told her that the tertiary was

Gisla, and that she was dead and wanted their prayers.[1]
A few weeks later the precious crown which Gisla
had laid down at St. Dominic's feet before she died
was brought to Catherine by one of her vassals from
Eggertsnaes. It was sold, and the proceeds sufficed
to maintain for a whole year the household and the
poor Scandinavians who were dependent upon them.

One evening, when the inmates of St. Bridget's
house were singing the *Ave Maris Stella*, they were
surprised by the arrival of the Prior of Alvastra,
Father Peter Olafson, who had come on a pilgrimage
to the tomb of the Apostles, and had fallen among
thieves on the way. He arrived half dead with cold
and fatigue, despoiled of a great part of his clothing,
for when they had taken away his coat he had
offered them his cloak also.

From him St. Bridget learnt news of her country,
of Magnus II.' and his Court, and of her own family;
she learnt also how much of her former prophecies
with regard to Sweden had come true. The plague
had entered Norway in a mysterious manner, and
entire parishes had fallen victims to it. In 1350
Magnus had two favourites, who were called his good
and his bad angels: Israel Birgerson, St. Bridget's
brother, a very holy man, was the good genius, and
Bennet Algotson, a worthless man, the evil influence.
In 1351 Magnus had undertaken a war approved by
the Holy See against the Russians, who were perse-
cuting the Christians in Ingria and Carelia; and
Israel, who was engaged in fighting on the side of
Magnus, died at Riga.

[1] See 'Vita S. Catherinæ.'

St. Bridget had written to Magnus in very plain terms, threatening him with punishment if he did not reduce Bennet Algotson to the rank of a subject, but in vain; and now war had broken out between Magnus and his eldest son Eric, whose place in the kingdom, and apparently, also, in his father's affections, had been taken by this unworthy courtier. Charles, the Seneschal of Nericia, Bridget's eldest son, was fighting on the side of Eric against Magnus in this civil war; but whether the saint approved of this or not, she does not seem to have interfered. Charles had always been a source of great trouble to her, and he had now grieved her very much by taking her youngest daughter, Cecilia, away from the Dominican convent at Skening, and marrying her to a friend of his own and a courtier. This was a bitter disappointment to St. Bridget, and one of her greatest trials; for she had set her heart upon Cecilia being a nun, and is said to have felt it more than the death of her other daughter, Ingeborg, a Cistercian nun, who died young. Later on Cecilia was left a widow, and married a Court physician, who had cured the King of a dangerous malady, which had carried off his Queen. This marriage St. Bridget disapproved of as being a mésalliance for the daughter of a princess. Cecilia seems to have been a very good wife and mother, and died a holy death at Vadstena. Our Lord comforted St. Bridget for her disappointment about Cecilia by telling her that some married women were more acceptable and pleasing to Him than some nuns.

Soon after Gisla's death Charles married a third

time, and by this wife, Catherine Glysdotter, he had
two sons, one of whom is said to have been cured
of epilepsy by his grandmother's prayers. Charles,
however, seems to have cared very little for his
family, and to have led a gay, worldly life at Court or
under arms, and to have left them alone at Upland.

Peace was concluded after about a year between
Magnus and Eric, on condition that Eric shared his
father's throne, and was also crowned King. His
younger brother had been made King of Norway, a
step Bridget disapproved of strongly, but she had
remonstrated in vain with Magnus for making this
division of his kingdom. The peace did not last long,
and on war breaking out again Magnus and his Queen
Blanche, with their second son, Hakon, King of Norway, went into Denmark, and put themselves in the
power of Valdemar, whose daughter, Marguèrite, Hakon
married. This was also against St. Bridget's advice,
for she had told Magnus that she knew Valdemar to
be a wolf and the worst enemy of Sweden, but the
King paid no heed to her counsels.

Magnus and Eric were once more reconciled, but
not long after a terrible tragedy occurred. Eric and
his wife Beatrice were at a banquet, to which they had
been invited by the Queen Blanche, when, after drink-
ing some wine, Beatrice suddenly fainted and died,
and a few minutes afterwards Eric was seized with
mortal illness. In his death-struggles he accused his
mother of having poisoned him and Beatrice because
Bennet Algotson had been banished from Court by
Eric. The people believed in Blanche's guilt, and it was
generally thought that Algotson was her accomplice,

and he was assassinated by his wife's family in revenge for his intrigue with Blanche.

St. Bridget received many Revelations concerning all these things and the consequences of them, which she wrote down and sent to Magnus with a long letter, bidding him go to Avignon, and confess his many sins to the Pope; telling him that if he refused to submit to the Divine Will, his flatterers would separate themselves from him, his kingdom would be divided, and his days cut short. The Revelations and visions which the saint had at this time are couched in most mystical language, so that, perhaps, there was some excuse for Magnus treating them as fanatical utterances, though there was none for his persistence in his wickedness.

But if the language in which the saint described her supernatural experiences, which were, perhaps, beyond expression, was obscure, her prophecies to Magnus were nevertheless fulfilled. After Eric's death, King Valdemar of Denmark seized some Swedish provinces, which had formerly belonged to Denmark, which so enraged the Swedish nobility that they made it an excuse for calling King Hakon from Norway to act as co-regent with his father in 1362; but when Hakon insisted upon marrying Valdemar's daughter Marguèrite, to whom he had been betrothed when she was only eleven, they rose and deposed Magnus and Hakon in favour of Albert of Mecklenburg, the nephew of Magnus. This was not accomplished without a severe struggle; but in 1365 Albert, after a decisive victory, mounted the throne. Hakon managed to escape by flight, but Magnus was taken prisoner, and remained for six years in captivity. He at length obtained his liberty by paying a heavy ransom and yielding all his rights to Albert. He passed the last years of his life in Norway, and was drowned near Bergen in 1374.

St. Bridget's eldest daughter Martha had in the meanwhile succeeded to her mother's former post as mistress of the palace, and had brought up with her own daughter Ingegard Hakon's betrothed, Marguèrite; but her method, though customary in those days, was not successful with either of the girls. Marguèrite rebelled against the rod, which was Martha's means of persuasion, and Ingegard became deceitful.

Father Peter of Alvastra would seem to have reached Rome about the time that the Swedish nobles, including St. Bridget's son Charles and her nephew, the Seneschal of Upland, were offering the Swedish crown to Albert of Mecklenburg; and though the great Swedish mystic appears to have known by revelation much that had happened, and that was going to happen, to her beloved Sweden, still he was able to supply many details and to confirm the truth of some of her visions by narrating what had actually occurred.

Father Peter was undoubtedly a very welcome arrival, for he it was who helped St. Bridget by translating her Revelations into Latin after writing them down from her dictation.

CHAPTER XIII

HER PILGRIMAGES IN ITALY

'Favour is deceitful, and beauty is vain; the woman that feareth the Lord, she shall be praised.'—Prov. xxxi. 30.

MANY of the religious questions of the time in which St. Bridget lived are treated of in her Revelations. A great controversy had been raging for some time among the Franciscans—who were divided into two parties, the Spirituals and the Conventuals—as to whether Our Lord and the Apostles possessed personal property, or whether they had all things in common. Pope John XXII. (1316-1334),[1] in his famous Decree, had already condemned the Fraticelli, a section of the Spirituals who maintained that a Friar Minor could not have any property, not even his own food, and had ordered them to submit their judgment to that of their superiors, and said :[2] 'Poverty is great, chastity is greater, and obedience is superior to both.' But the controversy among the Franciscans still continued in St. Bridget's time, and a Franciscan Friar consulted her upon this very point, and she replied that Our Lady had told her in a vision that the only thing Our Lord possessed of His own was the seamless garment

[1] 'L'Histoire Générale de l'Église,' par l'Abbé Darras, vol. iii.
[2] *Ibid.*

which she had woven for Him, and of which David had spoken in prophecy, saying, 'For My vesture they cast lots'; and the saint told the friar to observe that David did not say, 'For *Our* vesture.'

Another question which was raised by the Beguins and Fraticelli in the fourteenth century was as to what authority was possessed by bad Popes, and whether the ministrations of bad priests were valid. On both these points St. Bridget had so much to say in the Revelations that some Protestants have looked upon her as a forerunner of the so-called Reformation, though she was nothing of the kind. Severe as she was in rebuking the clergy, no matter how highly placed, for their sins, her writings were always in agreement with the doctrine of the Church, and she was much too well instructed in religion not to know that the unworthiness of the priest does not hinder the grace of the Sacraments. Such, briefly, was her answer to this question.

Yet another subject of frequent debate and dispute at this time was the ultimate fate of the heathen after death. Upon this question St. Bridget has a very sensible remark in the sixth book of her Revelations. She says : 'It is better for our own salvation to say one " Our Father " thoughtfully and simply than to dispute over such intricate questions, in the most sophistical manner, for the sake of winning a name in the world.'

When we consider that, in addition to all the hours St. Bridget spent in prayer and good works, she was also occupied with the politics of her country, and interested in all these questions, which involved deep theological reading to fit her to unravel them (though, of course, some of her knowledge was infused), it is clear that her time in Rome was very fully occupied; for, besides all this, the Rule and Constitutions of her Order filled much of her thoughts, and she must have gladly welcomed Father Peter of Alvastra, who helped her in translating the Revelations into Latin, and writing them down from her dictation. Besides all this, during the fourteen years that St. Bridget lived in Rome with St. Catherine, before the great work of bringing the Pope back from Avignon was accomplished, they spent a great deal of time in visiting the seven great basilicas, the Catacombs, and all the celebrated holy places in the city, over and over again. St. Bridget loved the Catacombs, and delighted in taking Catherine through them, and evidently had a passionate love for the Eternal City. She was often rapt in ecstasy in the churches. Sometimes she was raised in the air, sometimes she traversed space in a miraculous manner, and was often seen in Rome to run without touching the ground.[1] One of her favourite haunts was the beautiful basilica of St. Paul, a magnificent church with a nave and four aisles, sustained by columns taken from old pagan temples; here, too, was, and still is, the doubly famous crucifix—famous because tradition says that it spoke to St. Bridget as she knelt before it here, and famous also as a work of art, sculptured by the celebrated artist, Peter Cavallini.

[1] Flavigny, p. 329. This authoress quotes a number of writers, who say the saint was often seen to be borne through the air from St. John's to St. Peter's, and from the Vatican to St. Paul's-outside-the-Walls (p. 330).

St. Bridget is said to have frequently healed the sick in these visits to churches ; she was well known in the city, and venerated as a wonder-worker, as well as for her charity. St. Catherine's visits, as we have said, had to be regulated by her mother's supernatural knowledge. On October 4th, St. Francis's Day, 1364, St. Bridget was praying in the Church of San Francesco in Ripa, when the saint appeared to her and said : 'Come and eat and drink with me in my cell.' St. Bridget considered this as an invitation to go to Assisi, and spent many months in preparation for gaining the indulgence of the 'Portiuncula' there. In the following year, at the end of July, a Scandinavian pilgrimage, with St. Bridget at its head, set out from Rome for Assisi. Among the pilgrims were, of course, Father Peter of Alvastra, Father Peter of Skening, Catherine, and some faithful Swedish servants, who had followed either Bridget or Catherine to Rome. There was also the Bishop of Vexio, and Christine de Tofta, the mother of Bridget's nephew, the Seneschal of Upland. These two last had recently arrived from Sweden, bringing with them the news of the defeat and capture of Magnus, and the further intelligence that Hakon had been seriously wounded, although he had managed to escape to Norway. St. Bridget determined to make intercession for the repentance and liberation of Magnus, and this was one of the principal objects of her pilgrimage.

The pilgrims started on foot, with St. Bridget, staff in hand, and a little wooden cross on her breast, at their head, leaving the city by the Porta del Popolo. Rapt in prayer, St. Bridget saw none of the vast

plains and deserts through which she led the others;
neither the beauty of the scenery nor the majestic
ruins they passed had any attraction for her—in fact,
we cannot help thinking the saint was by no means
an ideal travelling companion, oblivious as she was of
fatigue and hunger, and apt to fall into an ecstasy
when others were longing for supper; though we may
not go so far as the cynic who said, 'The saints were
gey hard to live with.'

One night, when they were near Assisi, Catherine
was nearly captured by brigands, who, catching sight
of her by the fires the pilgrims had lit in their place
of encampment for the night, had exclaimed, ' Venus !'
St. Bridget, learning in prayer of their intention,
implored Our Lord to protect her daughter, and a
terrible storm arose, which so frightened the brigands
that they took to flight. The next day the pilgrims
reached Assisi, and were delighted with the wondrous
church, on whose walls Giotto and Cimabue have
painted, in fresco, the history of St. Francis.

The five days the pilgrims spent at Assisi were not
without trouble as well as great consolation for
St. Bridget; she was grieved to find that the Friars
Conventual had introduced relaxations of the Rule,
given to the Order by their holy founder, especially
with regard to poverty. The dispute between the
Conventuals and the Observants was now at its height,
and at the sacred convent of the Conventuals she
heard it all discussed, and was pained at the controversy, for if the Conventuals had erred in the
direction of laxity, the Observants had gone into the
other extreme. Certain learned men, too, had cast

doubt on the genuineness of the Portiuncula indulgence, declaring that it was a fiction which cast a gloom over the Scandinavian pilgrims, who had come so far to gain it. St. Bridget was rapt in ecstasy, in which she heard Our Lord say, 'I have granted to love what love has asked of Me,' and had from henceforth no doubt as to the indulgence, if, indeed, she had ever doubted. Before leaving the shrine of St. Francis, St. Bridget decided, with the consent of her confessors, to prolong her pilgrimage, and told her companions that she was going to visit the principal sanctuaries of the country before returning to Rome.

This pilgrimage lasted over two years. From Assisi they went to Ortona, near Arezzo. From Ortona they proceeded to Monte Gargane, a place which had long been celebrated as having been the scene of an apparition of St. Michael the Archangel, and here, as St. Bridget mounted the hill to the sanctuary, she was rapt in ecstasy, and felt herself surrounded by angels, and heard their song. After performing their devotions in the Church of St. Michael, the pilgrims descended the mountain to Manfredonia, where the Bishop of Vexio met with an accident. He had chosen to ride on horseback, as more consistent with his dignity, and on account of his bad health, but on going down this steep ascent his horse fell, and the Bishop broke two of his ribs. The pilgrims were to start very early the next morning for Barlatta, to avoid some corsairs who infested the coast; but the Bishop was in too much pain to start, and, at the same time, was afraid to remain alone at Manfredonia, so he sent for St. Bridget, and implored

her for the love of Our Lord to touch his side, and
he would cease to suffer. St. Bridget burst into tears,
and declared that she was nothing, but suggested that
they should pray together, and God would answer
them according to His Will. Kneeling down, she
prayed, and then laid her hand upon the Bishop's
side, and the pain at once left him, and he rose and
resumed the journey with the other pilgrims.

From Manfredonia they went to Bari to visit the
shrine of St. Nicholas, and from thence to Benevento,
where the relics of St. Bartholomew were enshrined.[1]
The Bishop was again taken very seriously ill with an
internal complaint, and again sent for St. Bridget,
and was once more healed.

On their way to Naples they met a friend of
St. Bridget's, Nicholas Orsini, who joined them, and
would fain have received them in his palace at Nola,
near Naples, but St. Bridget preferred to accept the
hospitality of the Seigneur of Buondelmonte and his
wife, Jacqueline Acciajuoli, who led an austere life, but
were in touch with the Court of Naples, where the
saint had work to do.

The beautiful young Queen, Joanna I. of Naples,
though still only a girl in years, had had a very
unhappy and romantic career. She had been most
unjustly accused of murdering her first husband,
Andrew of Hungary, and then, without waiting for
the necessary dispensation from Rome, had married
her cousin, Louis of Tarento, who was said to have
been her accomplice in murdering Andrew. In the

---

[1] These relics had been translated from the Lipari Isles in
839. In 1358 they were moved into a new church built for
them in Benevento (*Boll.*, August, vol. v., p. 43).

judgment of Pope Clement VI. she was innocent of this
crime, but she was constantly accused of it. Petrarch
and Boccacio defended her against those who believed
her guilty. Louis of Tarento did not live long after
his marriage with Joanna, and she married a third
time, just before the Scandinavian pilgrims reached
Naples, and this time also she did not wait for the
Holy See to sanction her marriage. On hearing of
St. Bridget's presence at the palace Buondelmonte,
the beautiful young Queen expressed a wish to see
her, and the saint went to the royal palace. The
Queen, who, in spite of her worldliness, had a strong
faith, listened to the counsels of the Swedish mystic
for a time, but after the saint had left Naples, she
forgot all her good resolutions, and relapsed into her
old habits. But while the saint was at Buondelmonte
it became the fashion for the courtiers, who idolized
the Queen, and followed her lead, to resort thither to
listen to St. Bridget, and to visit the poor and sick.

One lasting conversion of a celebrated young
Neapolitan nobleman, Eleazar, son of the Count of
Ariano, St. Bridget made at Naples, and this rich
young man gave up all to become a priest; he was
ultimately made a Cardinal by Pope Urban VI., and
was a zealous worker for the canonization of St.
Bridget. In the month of August, 1367, the pilgrims
returned to Rome, after a pilgrimage which had lasted
more than two years, and a few months after her
arrival in the Campo del Fiori the saint was to see
the return of the Pope to Rome, which had been one
of her principal intentions in all her prayers at the
various holy places she had visited.

CHAPTER XIV

THE RETURN OF THE POPE TO ROME

'Lord, Thou hast blessed Thy land: Thou hast turned away the captivity of Jacob.'—Ps. lxxxiv. 1.

IN 1362 a French Benedictine, Guillaume de Grisac, had ascended the throne of Peter under the title of Urban V., and in 1367 this Pope left Avignon and embarked at Marseilles for Italy. He said his first Mass in that country on the shore at Corneto, under the clear blue sky, with an enormous crowd to assist at it. On October 16, riding on a white horse, led by Italian princes and followed by eleven French cardinals, and accompanied by a procession of more than two thousand ecclesiastics—bishops, abbots, and priors—he entered Rome, to be received with the greatest joy by the Romans, who sang hymns, and acclaimed him with shouts of 'Evviva il Papa!' while the church bells rang joyfully. He entered the Vatican palace after giving the blessing, 'Urbi et Orbi,' from St. Peter's, and sang Mass on October 31 at the high altar; this was the first Mass sung there by a Pope since Boniface VIII.

St. Bridget lost no time in seeking an audience, and related a vision she had had which had miraculously told her of his return. In the course of this relation she entreated the Pope, in almost imperative terms, to reform the clergy, and to do away with the abuses which had crept into the Church, and to counsel all the bishops to act with prompt severity against simony and other sins into which the clergy had fallen, and which were scandalizing all good Catholics. The French Pope was a holy, wise, and austere man, who did not neglect the warnings and counsels of the Swedish saint, but at once set to work to repress the abuses, especially simony, which were bringing discredit on the Church.

On October 21 the prophecy of St. Bridget, made many years previously, that the Pope and Emperor would meet in Rome was fulfilled, for on that day the Emperor Charles IV. entered Rome, and, with the Duke of Savoy, led the white palfrey on which the Pope rode to St. Peter's on November 1, where the Emperor assisted at the Mass of Urban V., and the Pope crowned the Empress in the presence of an immense crowd. While the Emperor was in Rome St. Bridget placed the Rule and Constitutions of her Order in the hands of the Pope for his approval, in the presence of Charles, begging them to examine them. Urban evaded her request, and the Emperor left Rome without paying any attention to it, probably looking upon the Swedish Princess as a fanatical visionary, for he had at Viterbo received a letter from her, telling him, in the name of Our Lord, to examine the Rule which He had revealed to her.

Shortly after this another Swedish pilgrimage reached Rome, and among the pilgrims were Charles

and Birger, St. Bridget's two elder sons, the widow
of her nephew Ulf Sparre, of Upland, and the Bishop
of Vexio. Charles, the Seneschal of Nericia, had left
his third wife, for whom he did not care, in Sweden
with his children, and Birger was now a widower.
It was twenty years since St. Bridget had seen her
sons, and the meeting was not without drawbacks, for
she saw at a glance that Charles was ill, and as she
embraced him he broke a blood-vessel, but contact
with his mother healed him miraculously. Ulf's
widow, Catherine de Tofta, died not long after her
arrival in Rome.

The saint and her sons and their fellow-pilgrims had
a private audience of Urban V., at which Charles,
who loved splendour, was dressed in a coat of mail
covered with a mantle of ermine, and wearing a
magnificent massive silver belt, which attracted the
attention of His Holiness, for it was enriched with
precious stones.

The Pope looked at the two Swedish noblemen, and
then said to Birger : ' You are evidently the son of
your mother ;' and then, turning to Charles, he added :
' And you are a son of the world."

St. Bridget threw herself at the feet of the Sovereign
Pontiff, and cried : ' Give my sons absolution from
their sins.'

The Pope touched Charles's belt and said ironically :
' To carry these heavy clothes is, I suppose, a sufficient
penance.'

Some of the natural haughtiness of the Swedish
Princess peeped out in St. Bridget's answer. She
looked straight at His Holiness, and said respectfully :

'Most Holy Father, take away his sins, and I will undertake to take away his belt.'

Shortly after this, to the great disappointment of St. Bridget, the Pope left Rome for Viterbo, and took up his residence sometimes there, and sometimes in the gloomy castle of Montefiascone, longing to return to Avignon, his native country, yet reluctant to leave Italy. St. Bridget, with her two sons and her constant companion, Catherine, now started for a pilgrimage to Amalfi, accompanied by the Bishop of Vexio, the Prior of Alvastra, and Father Peter of Skening. Urban V. had given the two Swedish saints permission to have Mass said on a portable altar on their travels, so they were able to enjoy this privilege, even in places lying under an interdict. He had also enriched with an indulgence of a hundred days for each bead what is now known as the Brigittine Rosary, for in those days the Dominican Rosary was not in general use, except in the Dominican Order, people saying their beads according to their own private devotion. St. Bridget's custom was to say sixty-three *Aves* in honour of the years of Our Lady's life, seven 'Our Fathers' in memory of the seven dolours and joys of the Blessed Virgin, and instead of the *Glorias* of the present Rosary, seven *Credos*.

The pilgrims reached Amalfi at the end of Advent, and here Charles and Birger, the Bishop of Vexio, and the Prior of Alvastra, separated from the others and returned to Sweden, while St. Bridget, Catherine, and Father Peter of Skening went again to Naples, and did not go back to Rome till the spring of 1370. Here the news greeted the saint that the Pope was contemplating a return to Avignon, where his heart appears to have been, and shortly afterwards he left Rome for ever, going to Montefiascone. St. Bridget would fain have gone after him, to prevent him from going back to Avignon, but Our Lord sent her to Montefiascone on a very different errand.

'Go to the Pope; he is good, and would be a useful instrument if he did not allow himself to be imprisoned in worldly cares. Tell him that his time is short, that he must think of the salvation of the souls confided to his care. Say I have presented you with a Rule dictated by God for the Order which is to be founded at Vadstena. Jesus Christ wills that you should confirm it. As a spiritual dowry you shall bestow upon the monastery the indulgences which the Church of St. Peter in Vincula enjoys.' Thus, according to the Revelations, did Our Lord speak to the saint in one of her ecstasies, and as she was always prompt to obey the Voice she heard, she started at once, with the holy Bishop of Jaen, Alphonsus of Vadaterra, as her escort, for the Castle of Montefiascone, where she was joined by her friend Nicolas Orsini, who undertook to act as her interpreter, since her Northern accent and her very mystical language would make it difficult for the French Pope to understand her. The result of this interview was a Bull, addressed to the Bishops of Strengnase and Vexio, approving in a general way of the Constitutions of the Order of St. Saviour, and authorizing the completion of the convent for nuns, already in course of construction at Vadstena, and the building of a monastery for monks in the same place. In this interview St. Bridget promised the

THE RETURN OF THE POPE TO ROME 109

Sovereign Pontiff, who suffered from melancholy, great spiritual joys from time to time, and soon after her return to Rome the Pope's confessor went to see her, and told her her prediction had been fulfilled, and the Pope was inundated with spiritual consolations, and asked the saint for revelations concerning the Divine Will. Urban died in the odour of sanctity at Avignon that same year, and was afterwards beatified. He was buried temporarily at Marseilles, in the Abbey of St. Victor, having finished his days in the practice of great penance and humility. He was noted for his charity and justice.

Ten days after, Cardinal de Beaufort was elected to the Chair of Peter, under the title of Gregory XI., to the discontent of the Romans, for he was the seventh of the French Cardinals who had occupied the Papal See; but with him St. Bridget's hopes of seeing the Pope return permanently revived, though they were not destined to be fulfilled in her lifetime. She sent three most urgent letters to Avignon, warning him to return, which, though they made him so uneasy that he twice sent his Nuncio to confer with her on her Revelations, did not have the desired effect until after St. Bridget had been dead four years. At last he transferred the Papal See from Avignon to Rome in 1377.[1]

On May 21, 1371, St. Bridget had a vision, in which Our Lord commanded her to prepare to make a pilgrimage to Jerusalem, that Holy Land which Our Lady, twenty years before, had told her she should one day see. But now that which had once been the desire of her life was to be accomplished she

[1] *Boll.*, October, vol. iv., p. 429.

no longer desired it—a not uncommon experience in a
world where things, not always, but sometimes, come
too late. She was getting old, her health was enfeebled
by her austerities, and she would rather have remained
in Rome than undertake this long and painful pilgrimage; but she could not disobey what she felt to be the
Voice of Our Lord, and she at once began to make
preparations for the journey.

In the autumn of that year Charles and Birger, her
two sons; Father Peter, the Prior of Alvastra; the old
Bishop of Jaen; a Spanish nun; the Chevalier Magnus
of Eka; and the Swedish chaplain, Frederick Gudmar-
son, all arrived in Rome to join the pilgrimage, which
started immediately upon their arrival.

CHAPTER XV

ST. BRIDGET IN THE HOLY LAND

'Her children rose up, and called her blessed; her husband, and he praised her.'—Prov. xxxi. 27.

The Swedish pilgrims sailed from Ostia for Naples in a small Genoese vessel, manned by slaves and Orientals, and with very poor accommodation for passengers. The ladies' cabin was a little, dark, airless place, in which they had to pass the greater part of the day, as well as the night, for it was contrary to the custom of the age for the women to take their meals on deck with the others. Just before sailing, St. Bridget turned to Father Peter of Alvastra, and said: 'We shall all return safely except the one I love the best'—words which proved prophetic, as we shall see.

On their arrival at Naples, St. Bridget was treated with the greatest honour, for she was already revered there as a saint; but the pilgrims refused the offers of hospitality made them by the Neapolitan nobility, and took up their quarters in the hospice of Santa Maria d'Avvocata, attached to the convent of the Knights Hospitallers of St. John of Jerusalem.

The beautiful Neapolitan Queen, Joanna I., had just returned from a visit to the Pope at Avignon,

111

where Gregory XI. had received her very graciously, and St. Bridget at once sought an interview with her, to hear the latest news of the Pope's plans, and whether he was likely to return to Rome soon.

No more extraordinary incident than the one we are now about to describe illuminates with the lamp of romance the pages of history. Joanna, though now nearly forty-five, was still supremely beautiful, a very tall, fine woman, with golden hair and large black eyes, a lovely complexion, and fine, well-cut features, a statuesque type of face, and any ravages that time might have made were repaired by art. She was, of course, magnificently attired, and was surrounded by courtiers, who idolized ' the Light of Italy,' as Petrarch called her, but she was known all over Europe as ' the sweet Queen.'

The Swedish Princess presented her two sons to the Queen. Birger, the younger, behaved properly, and knelt and kissed Joanna's hand, but the handsome Charles, his mother's darling son, was struck speechless by the Queen's wonderful beauty, and evinced his admiration by stepping impulsively forward and kissing her on the lips before the whole Court. The Neapolitan courtiers were naturally furious at such conduct, and seized their swords, and would have made short work of this handsome but impertinent young Swede, noble though he was, but the Queen restrained them, and, far from disapproving or resenting Charles's bold insolence, made up her mind to marry him. Her third husband, King James of Majorca, had disappeared in a recent Spanish war, and the Queen believed herself to be a widow for the third time. But if there were no obstacle on her side to marriage with Charles, there was a very serious one on his part, for he had a wife in Sweden, of whom he would have fain been rid.

St. Bridget retired from this audience stricken with grief, and cast herself at Our Lord's feet in the chapel of the convent, adjoining the hospice. In vain she represented to Joanna that Charles was not free to marry her. The Queen was determined to have Charles; she heaped presents upon him, and he abandoned the pilgrimage to the Holy Land, and decided to remain in Naples, marry the Queen, and trust to her influence with the Pope to get a dispensation to enable him to do so, which he foolishly persuaded himself the Holy See was able to grant him. St. Bridget was, of course, horror-struck at such wickedness, but her authority over her son was powerless against the spell the beauty of the Queen had cast over him, so she had recourse to prayer, her unfailing remedy in all her troubles.

On February the 24th the Queen gave a grand ball, and as Charles, for whom she was waiting, did not appear, she sent her chamberlain to see what had detained him. He found the Lord of Nericia stricken with a mortal illness, described in St. Bridget's biographies as fever, though this does not convey much information as to the real nature of the attack, which proved fatal. St. Bridget and Catherine spent the next fortnight by his bedside, where they had the happiness of seeing him turn to God in repentance for his sins before he died. The Bishop of Jaen gave him the consolations of religion, and Our Blessed Lady consoled his heart-broken mother in a vision in which she assured her that Charles's soul was saved, partly through his mother's prayers, partly through his own devotion to Our Lady, for whom he would have died at any time of his life.

After burying Charles at Naples with the great pomp commanded by Joanna, the pilgrims set sail for Cyprus on March the 10th, 1372. They spent a few days in Messina waiting for a fair wind, mostly in the churches, for they were unable to have Mass on board ship, and on Good Friday, an unlucky day according to sailors, they resumed their voyage. A violent tempest broke over them soon after leaving Messina, but they reached Cyprus safely, and here St. Bridget preached to a large crowd outside the cathedral, many of whom scoffed and laughed at her, especially the Genoese merchants, who formed a large contingent of her audience. She made, however, two notable converts, both of whom joined the pilgrimage—an Englishman named William Williamson, and a Franciscan friar named Martin of Aragon, secretary to the Queen of Cyprus. Between Cyprus and Jaffa the ship in which the pilgrims were sailing was wrecked, and they were in imminent danger of being drowned. A terrible scene took place on board: not only all the cargo, but also all the pilgrims' luggage, was thrown overboard to lighten the sinking vessel. Bishop Alphonsus of Vadaterra fetched St. Bridget and her companions up from the wretched little cabin to the deck, where all was confusion, and the screams of the frightened passengers and crew deafening. St. Bridget was calm and composed, and, with her arms round

Catherine, assured the Bishop of Jaen that no one
would perish; and so it turned out, for they were all
safely landed at Jaffa in small boats. Jaffa is still
the most difficult of all ports to make, and, indeed, it
can only be made in certain stages of the tides and in
certain winds, and it is sometimes days, and even
weeks, before passengers can be landed. Once arrived
in the Holy Land, St. Bridget seems to have passed
her time in a series of ecstasies and visions, all of
which are recorded in her Revelations. At Bethlehem
she had a vision, long promised by Our Lady, of the
Nativity; at Calvary, of the Crucifixion; in Jerusalem,
of the Scourging; at the Church of the Holy Sepulchre,
of the Resurrection; at Damascus, of the Martyrdom
of St. Stephen, who appeared to her; at Nazareth, of
the Immaculate Conception of the Blessed Virgin. On
the banks of the River Jordan she saw in vision Our
Lord walking as He did in His lifetime, the most
beautiful of all the sons of men; at Jerusalem she
saw the upper chamber, with Our Lady and all the
Apostles, except the traitor. All she saw and heard
she told to Alphonsus of Vadaterra and Father Peter
of Alvastra, and the Prior translated it into Latin.

It is not surprising that this visit to the Holy Land
should have been so prolific in visions and ecstasies to
the great Swedish mystic; the supreme desire of her
life was realized as she rode or walked over its sacred
soil, sanctified for ever as it is by the footsteps of God
Incarnate, who, to fulfil His own promise, chose this
land of all other lands on the face of the earth to
honour with His blessed presence. All St. Bridget's
former meditations and contemplations on the life

8—2

and passion of Our Divine Lord, and on the joys and sorrows of His Blessed Mother, were now, as it were, actually taking place before her eyes, for to the mystic neither time nor space exist.

Her emotional nature had been strained almost to breaking-point by the intense grief which her eldest son Charles's death had caused her, and perhaps Our Divine Lord permitted this great sorrow to befall His spouse on the eve of her entrance to the Holy Land in order to prepare and predispose her to receive the marvellous consolations He vouchsafed to bestow upon her during this pilgrimage. Even ordinary mortals are brought nearer to the unseen world in times of great grief, and their perceptions of spiritual things are sharpened by sorrow; much more would a temperament like St. Bridget's be more susceptible of mystical impressions when her soul was crushed and wounded by the loss of her eldest son and favourite child. She seems to have felt this trial even more acutely than she did the death of her husband Ulf, and only the assurance of Our Lady that Charles's soul was safe enabled her to bear this anguish as she did.

The last place she appears to have visited in Palestine was the Garden of Gethsemane, where, at the foot of the Mount of Olives, Catherine also received consolation; and, on leaving it, St. Bridget announced that the pilgrimage was over, and that Our Lord had bidden her to return to Rome. The pilgrims had been eight months in the Holy Land, when, in the month of September, they embarked at Jaffa for Cyprus, where they arrived safely at Famagusta, on October 8.

Our Lord had revealed to St. Bridget that this place was a second Gomorrah, and she determined to seek an interview with the Queen and Princes to warn them of the judgments which were coming upon them as a punishment for their pride and wickedness, as she had done on her former visit to Cyprus, and also by her letters from Jerusalem. The King of Cyprus, Peter the Great, had recently been assassinated—it was believed, by his brothers, John and James of Antioch; some said with the connivance of his wife, the Queen-mother Eleanor, whose child was about to be crowned under the title of Peter II. when the Swedish pilgrims reached Cyprus.

The palace was filled with all the highest nobility of the kingdom for this ceremony, when St. Bridget visited it, and, before them all, she denounced the two Princes, James and John, and the Queen-mother, warning them that, unless they repented of the murder of the late King, God would, as He had revealed to her, punish them severely. Far from listening to her exhortations, the Princes treated her as a mad woman, and paid no attention to her warnings. Nothing daunted by the contempt she met with in the palace, Bridget went into the city and preached in the public places to the people, publishing all the revelations she had received at Jerusalem concerning Cyprus and the fall of Constantinople, which last seemed to her hearers too ridiculous to consider seriously. And the people in the streets, like the nobles in the palace, refused to listen, and said: 'Let us prepare for the coronation instead of listening to this old woman in her dotage.'

Finding all her efforts, both private and public, to convert the Royal Family and people of Cyprus were in vain, St. Bridget left for Naples on October the 17th, 1372. Here we may mention that all her prophecies were fulfilled concerning the island and the Royal House of Lusignan, which, after the assassination of John of Antioch by the Queen Eleanor—as it was said, in revenge for her husband's death—disappears from the pages of history.

CHAPTER XVI

DEATH OF ST. BRIDGET

'Precious in the sight of the Lord is the death of His saints.'
—Ps. cxv. 15.

WE must not forget to mention a great joy St. Bridget
received in the Holy Land, in connection with her
second son, Birger. Before the pilgrims left Jerusalem
he was made a Knight of the Holy Sepulchre, and
made his vows in the hands of a Franciscan friar, to
the great consolation of his holy mother. The health
of St. Bridget began to fail in Palestine, and on the
voyage to Cyprus her two children, Birger and
Catherine, were very anxious about her; she appeared
to be wasting away, and lost all appetite, and was
also suffering from fever, and no doubt from nervous
exhaustion, the reaction after all the ecstasies and
raptures she had experienced in the Holy Land. Her
austerities, and the privations and fatigue of travel,
had told upon her fragile frame, for she was turned
seventy, and could no longer bear with impunity the
strain which all these mystical experiences imposed
on her physical system. She had for eight months
been leading the life of an angel in the weak, suffering
body of a woman who had already seen her three
score years and ten—no wonder that she was now in a

state of collapse. She revived sufficiently at Cyprus
to perform the work she believed Our Lord had set
her to do there, but her want of success must have
dispirited her. On arriving at Naples, they found
that lovely city ravaged by the plague, which was
raging there, and the saint was received by the Queen,
the Archbishop of Naples, and a great crowd of the
people, all imploring her to beg Almighty God to save
them from this terrible scourge. She answered them
that penitence was the only thing that availed to turn
away the anger of God, but added that she would
pray for light, and tell them what message Our Lord
had for them. She wrote a letter to Joanna I., urging
her to repent and confess her sins, and she had several
private interviews with the beautiful but much-
maligned Queen, in which the saint did not spare her
warnings and threats of Divine punishment, though
whether they had any permanent effect on the Queen
seems doubtful. St. Bridget also wrote to the Archbishop, and had her letter translated into Latin, and
taken to him by the hand of Magnus of Eka ; in this
letter she denounced the horrible sins and vices of the
Neapolitans, declaring that they added to them by
abandoning themselves to pagan superstitions, and
encouraging sorcerers and enchanters, and warning
him that, unless the people repented, they would be
hated by God.

The saint received other revelations concerning
Naples and its people, which she also communicated
to Bernard, the Archbishop, and he had them read
from the pulpits to large congregations in the
churches, and sermons preached upon them to the

laity, and also to the Canons, theologians, and doctors of canon law, to whom Alphonsus read the text of the Revelations in Latin. Various miracles are reported to have taken place in Naples by St. Bridget's means, which helped to enforce her words and give weight to them.[1] Many conversions were made, but mostly among the clergy and upper classes; the masses seem to have paid no attention to these discourses, being too ignorant to understand them, for the neglect of instructing the ignorant in the Faith was one of the sins for which the saint had come to rebuke the clergy.

At the request of the Queen and Archbishop of Naples, St. Bridget stayed two months in the city, but she was ill most of the time, and further embarrassed by want of means to continue her journey to Rome. Neither Catherine nor Birger had had any pecuniary aid from Sweden, so they could not help her, and she did not want to put herself under obligations to the Queen by borrowing of her. Finally, a sum of money was sent her anonymously, which she suspected to come from Joanna, but, after some hesitation, she accepted it, and the pilgrims left Naples for Rome in March, 1373, after two years' absence.

In January St. Bridget had sent a long letter from Naples to Avignon to the Pope, Gregory XI., which Alphonsus of Vadaterra translated into Latin, and himself took to Avignon and delivered. In it the saint told the Pope of the revelations she had received concerning him, and urged him in impassioned language to return to Rome as quickly as he could, to

---

[1] Flavigny, p. 473.

occupy his own episcopal see, warning him that later he would not have the physical strength to do so. All this revelation was delivered as the words of Our Lord Himself to the supreme Pontiff, warning, rebuking, threatening, and imploring him to come humbly back to Him, and promising to bless him eternally if he obeyed.

The Pope received the holy Bishop of Jaen most kindly, and kept him near him for some time; but, though he read and meditated upon the letter, he had not the moral or physical energy to act upon it at the time, and allowed himself to be persuaded by his French court to remain in Avignon.

The Swedish pilgrims had a good passage to Rome, but every day St. Bridget grew weaker, and the others almost feared she would not reach Rome alive. Lent had just begun when at length Bridget and her companions got safely back to the house in the Campo dei Fiori, and the saint, ill as she was, began to visit the churches of the stations. She also paid and received many visits, for the approach of death was already written upon her changed countenance, and from far and near people flocked to see the saint once more. The end, however, was not to be just yet. She continued her usual life of vigils, prayer, and visits to the holy places for some months, and then was obliged to remain in the house. She was now beset with various temptations, especially those which were most calculated to humble that pride which had always been the greatest obstacle to her perfection: she was assailed with all kinds of spiritual temptations, including doubts as to the mysteries of the

Faith; but these passed away, and again Our Blessed Lady appeared to her and comforted her. Besides her physical sufferings, which were very severe, her poverty at this time was so great that Catherine and Birger were obliged to borrow money from a Swedish tailor who was passing through Rome to procure the bare necessaries of life.

The saint lingered on until July, and on the 22nd of that month she called Catherine to her bedside, and foretold that her death would take place the next day, as in fact it did.

On the morning of the 23rd Father Peter of Alvastra said Mass very early in her cell, and communicated her. She had ordered them to clothe her in her hair-shirt, and to place her on a wooden table, and when Mass was over Father Peter of Skening anointed her, after which, as so often happens, she revived, and called all her family round her, till her cell was filled with visitors, who listened to her last words of exhortation with attention and emotion, knowing that they were the words of a saint. Father Magnus of Eka, who had been ordained priest since his return from the Holy Land, said a Mass of thanksgiving in her cell after the Sacrament of Extreme Unction had been administered, and at the elevation St. Bridget raised her head and cried in Latin: 'Lord, into Thy Hands I commend my spirit.' These were her last words, uttered, it is said, in a strong voice, about ten o'clock on the morning of July the 23rd, 1373.

She was in her seventy-first year when she died. She was not buried in the Brigittine habit, for she

had never worn it, but in the Franciscan, because she
had long been a Franciscan tertiary. She had left
instructions that she was to be taken to Vadstena and
interred in the new monastery, the first of the Order
of St. Saviour; but she had to be buried within twenty-
four hours in Rome, according to the custom of the
country, so it was decided by her children to take her
body to the convent of the Poor Clares of San Lorenzo,
in Panisperna, to be temporarily deposited there.[1]
But on arriving at the convent the crowd who desired
to venerate her remains was so great that the funeral
had to be delayed till the 26th, to enable the people
all to enter the church and pass before her coffin.

Contrary to the instructions and wish of the saint,
a grand procession of Cardinals, prelates, noblemen,
clergy, and laity had followed the body from her
house in the Campo dei Fiori to the convent in Panisperna. Here the sacred remains were enclosed in a
wooden coffin, and that was placed in a white marble
tomb in the Church of St. Laurence, attached to the
convent, lent by a noble Roman lady, a former friend
of the saint. But before it was temporarily interred
there several miracles were reported in the city to
have happened. One of the most striking was that
of a Roman lady, well known for an enormous goitre,
which disappeared completely on her touching the
body of St. Bridget.

The funeral took place at night, on July the 26th,
and the Church of St. Laurence was not large enough

[1] 'She had commanded them to bury her secretly by night;
but it happened quite otherwise, on account of the crowd'
(*Boll.*, October, p. 461).

to admit the crowd of all classes of people, from the
highest to the lowest, who thronged in at the doors.
Thank-offerings of every kind began to pour in, till
the chapel was filled with them. Among these was
a young Turkish captive of royal birth, or, as some
say, a Tartar princess, whom Joanna I. of Naples
sent, after she had liberated her in obedience to the
counsels of St. Bridget, who had remonstrated with
her for keeping slaves. This young girl was instructed
by Catherine and Birger, who had her baptized in
Rome, and they took her with them to Sweden, where
she afterwards became a nun at Vadstena.

As St. Bridget had left instructions in her will that
Catherine was to take her remains to Vadstena to
rest finally there, this was the first pious care of the
co-foundress of the Brigittines, but it was necessary to
consult first with the Bishop of Jaen, Alphonsus of
Vadaterra, as to ways and means, and he was still
detained by the Pope at Avignon; so, until he returned,
five weeks later, Catherine remained in her cell in
her late mother's house in Rome. Thus lived and
died a great woman, as well as a canonized saint of
the Church, recognized as the former still by her
Protestant countrymen and countrywomen, who, anti-
Catholic as the Swedes now are, make a point of
visiting her former house in the Campo dei Fiori
when they go to Rome. She still lives in her daughters
the Brigittines, who are her best memorial, for,
greater than all her political work, greater than her
labours as a reformer, was the foundation of the
Order destined to play such an important work as it
did in the conversion and religious life of Sweden,

until the Protestant Reformation drove it into exile. That it may one day, in the Providence of God, return to its native soil, and play a part in the reconversion of Sweden, is the daily prayer of the daughters of this venerable Order.

CHAPTER XVII

THE CRADLE AND THE GRAVE

'Her lamp shall not be put out in the night.'—PROV. xxxi.

So long as St. Bridget lived Catherine led a life of the greatest retirement, apparently under the direction of her mother and Father Peter of Skening; but after bearing the yoke so long, she now came forward, and from henceforth the mantle of St. Bridget appears to have fallen on her daughter, the beautiful, most sweet and amiable young widow. For the next seven years she laboured indefatigably for the canonization of her mother, which, however, she did not live to see accomplished.

No sooner did Alphonsus of Vadaterra return from Avignon to Rome than, on September 17, he, Catherine, Birger, Father Peter of Alvastra, Father Peter of Skening, and many Roman noblemen, went to St. Laurence's to open the tomb of St. Bridget, which they did in the presence of a great many witnesses. Nothing remained but the skeleton: all the flesh had disappeared; and at the sight, the spirit of St. Bridget seems to have animated Catherine, who, throwing back her veil, began to preach to the crowd, and is said to have made many conversions, which she attributed to her mother. After giving the Poor

127

Clares the bones of the left arm, as relics of the saint, the tomb was again sealed up, and Catherine and Birger and their followers made preparations for their journey with the relics to Sweden.

This took some time, as the money to defray the expenses of the journey had to be collected, and it was not until early in December that the Scandinavians left Rome amid an enormous crowd, who were loth to part with the relics of the saint that had lived so many years and finally died in their midst; but Vadstena had the first claim on her, and, moreover, it was in obedience to her last wishes that she was removed thither. They stopped first at Montefiascone, a beautiful and romantic hill-city, where the Papal Nuncio and the Bishop of the diocese examined the account of the life and miracles of their penitent, which the two Fathers, Peter of Skening and the Prior of Alvastra, handed them.

This was the first step in introducing the cause of St. Bridget, in working for which St. Catherine and her advisers showed great prudence as well as zeal. This first step taken, they embarked near Ancona for Trieste, and from thence they went overland through Austria and Poland to Danzig, where they remained some time. Their journey showed how widely spread was the fame of St. Bridget and her sanctity, for wherever they stopped the churches were gladly opened to receive her relics for a short time, and at Marienburg, in Prussia, the reception was a truly royal one which the Knights Hospitallers of St. John gave them. These Knights had come from the Holy Land to convert the Slavs and Prussians. Some of the

Hospitallers, together with two Roman prelates, accompanied the funeral train as far as Danzig, where they took leave of the Scandinavians, who embarked there for Sudercopia. They landed on June the 14th, and according to tradition, were guided by a star during the voyage. From Sudercopia they proceeded to Lincoping, the episcopal see of the diocese in which Vadstena stands.

Here they were met by the holy Bishop Hermanson, who at the head of the clergy was joined by a great crowd from all parts of Ostrogothia, to accompany the relics to Vadstena. St. Catherine, who at Danzig had preached to the people, addressed the crowds at all the towns they passed through between Sudercopia and Vadstena. At Lincoping all the bells rang out as they entered the city. They went with the relics to the cathedral, and after a service and a sermon a Chapter was held, at which St. Catherine with great reverence took the holy Bishop Hermanson to task for his austerities; for he had shut himself up for a long time, fasting and praying, to the detriment of his pastoral duties, and St. Catherine told him it would be more pleasing to God if he attended to them.

It is very remarkable how, after the death of her mother, St. Catherine came forward and played a very active part in teaching and preaching, as well as in working for the canonization of St. Bridget, and in establishing her Order. The personality of St. Bridget apparently completely overshadowed her daughter while she lived, and as soon as she was dead, we see what a capable woman St. Catherine also was. Her name is entered in the Roman Martyrology as a canonized saint (March 22), and though a few years ago a report came from the Brigittine convent at Weert, in Holland, that the Bull of her canonization had been found, the text of it appears to be no longer extant. The holy Bishop, far from resenting the exhortations of St. Catherine, whom he had known from a child, believed he heard her mother speaking through her lips, and promised to come out of his retreat and accompany the relics to Vadstena, as a preliminary step to returning to his episcopal duties.

The new monastery of St. Saviour was beautifully situated at Vadstena, on the shores of the great Lake Wetter. It was, of course, far from finished, and the large wooden church which divided the nuns' quarters from those of the monks was only a temporary building.

On July the 4th, a Thursday within the Octave of St. Peter and St. Paul, as the diary tells us, the relics of the holy foundress were solemnly brought into this church, and the next day exposed to the veneration of the faithful; while for a week people from the neighbouring districts came to visit the remains of the saint they had loved so much in her lifetime. Numerous miracles are reported to have occurred at the tomb, and the fame of the sanctity of St. Bridget began to spread all over the Christian world, and Vadstena became a celebrated place of pilgrimage.

The nuns and monks received St. Catherine with the greatest joy and affection, and at once acclaimed her as their first Abbess. She, who had served so

long and painful a novitiate at Rome, under the stern
guidance of Father Peter of Skening, would fain from
humility have entered the monastery as a simple
novice, but, fortunately, the Bishops of Vexio, Lincoping, and Strengnaes, with the Archbishop of Upsala,
overcame Catherine's scruples, and she entered on her
duties as Abbess. At the end of the week St. Bridget
was buried in the church, her son Birger and some of
the saint's best friends carrying the coffin; but a still
grander function was to take place a few years later,
when the Bull of canonization was at last published.

Meanwhile Catherine laboured to form her congregation, on the model her holy mother, their
foundress, set before her during the long years they
were in Rome. She set them all a perfect example
by observing most strictly every detail of their holy
rule, governing both houses with the greatest sweetness and patience, so that it was said no impatient
word was ever heard to proceed from her lips. Then
the number of the miracles attributed to St. Bridget
was so large that the King of Sweden, the prelates,
and the great men and the clergy of the kingdom,
with one voice decreed that it was time for St.
Catherine to go back to Rome, to labour for the
canonization of her mother; and at the command of
the Bishop of Lincoping, she set out in the spring
of 1375 once more for the Eternal City, accompanied
by Master Peter of Skening, Father Peter of Alvastra,
a chaplain and a lay-sister to wait upon her. They
arrived safely, and found that many Cardinals and
highly-placed people, who had known St. Bridget in
her lifetime, and could testify to her sanctity, were

strongly inclined to promote her cause. Catherine
brought with her petitions from the King, Lords, and
prelates of Sweden, begging humbly for the same
object. After staying some time in Rome, she
went to Naples to collect and write down all the
miracles the saint had performed there, both before
and after her death, and, on her return to Rome, she
had an audience of Gregory XI., who had left Avignon,
and returned to Rome on January 17, 1375. As the
Orsini had led the reins of the white charger on
which the Pope rode while entering the city, he said
to His Holiness, 'Most Holy Father, I understand
to-day the prophecy the holy Bridget made to me five
years ago, when she told me that not only should I
live to see you re-enter Rome, but also that I should
conduct you thither.'

Soon after the Pope's return, a terrible inundation
of the Tiber threatened to destroy the city, when,
upon the suggestion of one of St. Bridget's disciples,
the college of Cardinals and the Pope himself went to
her former house in the Campo dei Fiori, where
Catherine was staying, and begged her to save Rome.
Catherine humbly protested that she had no power
over the flood; but the people, unsatisfied with this
answer, dragged her in tears to the river, where, it
is said, at each step she made towards the banks
the water retreated before her. Father Peter of
Alvastra took advantage of this to demand the
canonization of Catherine's mother, knowing that
would please the daughter better than any tribute of
praise to herself. Catherine's own sanctity appears to
have weighed much with Gregory in granting her, as

he did in several audiences she had with him, many
favours for the Order of St. Saviour, and indulgences
and privileges for the monastery-church at Vadstena.

One of the most zealous promoters of the cause of
St. Bridget was John of Torquemada, who laid it
before Gregory XI. in 1377; but the death of the Pope,
on March the 27th of the following year, put a temporary stop to these measures. He was succeeded by
Bartholomew Prignani, the Archbishop of Bari, who
took the title of Urban VI. The new Pope received
Catherine in audience soon after his accession, and
remarked, on seeing her, that 'she had been nourished
with her mother's milk,' meaning that she was a true
daughter of Bridget.

Before the end of the year, the French Cardinals,
who had elected Urban to the Papal throne, withdrew
from him, and elected at Fondi an Antipope, under
the name of Clement VII. As soon as St. Catherine
heard it, she remembered that her mother had
predicted it, saying: 'This is the schism prophesied
by my mother.'

Besides the delay in the canonization, another trial
befell St. Catherine in the year 1378, in the death of
Father Peter of Skening, who had so long ruled the
house of St. Bridget in Rome, and directed both her
and St. Catherine, and was now Prior and Confessor-
General of the monastery at Vadstena. He fell from
the top of St. Bridget's house to the bottom, and from
that time his hand was paralyzed, and he was lame;
but he never complained, and was always patient and
resigned. He was so gentle and patient in ruling the
household in Rome, and the community at Vadstena,

that they looked upon him and venerated him, not so much as a teacher, but as a mother who comforted them in all their troubles. Most charitable and compassionate to the poor, he was very severe with himself, practising great austerities. His canonization was asked of Leo X., but the Protestant Reformation broke out, and put a stop to that as well as to many other causes.

CHAPTER XVIII

CONCLUSION

'Give her of the fruit of her hands; and let her works praise her in the gates.'—PROV. xxxi.

THE delay in the process of canonization caused by the Papal schism prolonged St. Catherine's stay in Rome, and while she was there she met St. Catherine of Siena, whom God had raised up to continue the work of bringing the Popes back from Avignon, for which St. Bridget had so zealously laboured. A greater contrast in every way than the dyer's daughter of Siena and the Swedish princess could hardly be found. The two saints had several interviews, in the course of which St. Catherine of Sweden learnt that St. Catherine of Siena worked upon the Popes in quite a different way from that of her mother. St. Bridget's principal means had been her gift of prophecy, while St. Catherine used all her eloquent powers of persuasion and her infused wisdom. She acted upon the reason and intellect of the Pontiffs, St. Bridget upon their consciences and affections. In the end, as everyone knows, it was the dyer's daughter who completed the work the Princess had begun.

Urban VI. was anxious to send the two Catherines on a mission to the Queen of Naples, Joanna I., who, annoyed by Urban's haughtiness, had joined the party of the Antipope. Catherine of Siena was ready to obey immediately the Pope expressed the wish, but Catherine of Sweden absolutely declined to visit Joanna again. She had refused to listen to the admonitions of her mother, and Catherine considered it would be useless for her to try to influence the beautiful but worldly and wilful Queen. Moreover, she was anxious to return to her monastery as soon as she could be spared from Rome, and on July the 6th, 1380, she arrived at Vadstena, to the mingled joy and sorrow of the community there—joy at seeing her again, sorrow because they saw she would not long be spared to them.

A miracle is reported to have been worked by Catherine soon after her return to Vadstena. One of the workmen fell from the roof of the new chapel, with which great progress had been made, as also with other buildings of the monastery, during the absence of the Abbess. The man, who was terribly injured, was brought to Catherine, who, her biographer says, cured him completely.

She lived nine months after her return from Rome, during which time she superintended the building of the monastery, and cared for the temporal and spiritual welfare of her subjects, instructing them in the holy Rule, and setting an example to all by her obedience, humility, and, as she got worse, by her patience, which edified everyone. She suffered continually various bodily pains, but the weaker she grew in body the more vigorous was her mind. She followed her mother's custom of confessing daily, as she had done ever since her return from the Holy

Land, and during her illness she sometimes humbly accused herself of her sins three or four times a day. Her illness did not permit her to receive Holy Communion, but the Blessed Sacrament was brought to her cell and shown to her. Finally, in the presence of her daughters, she fell asleep happily in the Lord on March the 22nd, 1381. It is said that, as she was dying, the birds came by thousands and perched on the windows of the monastery, filling the air with their melody. In those days it was piously and beautifully believed that the birds sing when a soul enters into glory.

Prince Eric, son of the King of Sweden, the Bishop of Strengnaes, her only surviving brother and sister, Birger and Cecilia, and a great crowd of nobles, were present at her funeral, before and after which many miracles are reported to have occurred.

She did not live to see the consecration of Vadstena Monastery, nor the canonization of her mother, but these events, for which she had longed so deeply and laboured so zealously, both took place after she had gone to her rest. She was succeeded as Abbess of Vadstena by her niece Ingeborg, the daughter of St. Bridget's eldest daughter, Martha. Ingeborg was brought up, as we have mentioned, with Queen Margaret, but did not do so much justice to her guardians as Margaret, who became a great Queen, for the new Abbess is described by her biographer as 'richer in dowry than in virtues,' and, although an enclosed nun, seems to have been a worldly-minded woman.

St. Bridget's other great friend and confessor,

Father Peter, the Prior of Alvastra, did not long
survive Catherine; he died, as we learn from the diary
of Vadstena, on April the 9th, 1390, and was brought
to his monastery to be buried, with great honour, by
Bishop Nicholas of Lincoping.   The other companion
of St. Bridget's pilgrimage, Father Gudmar, had died
the previous year.   A few days after Catherine's death
in 1388 a great fire broke out in her beloved monastery,
and completely destroyed the chapel, which was of
wood, and also a great part of the monastery; it
occurred in the middle of the night.   One of the lay-
brothers, Ingulphus by name, who had a great devotion
to Our Lady, and tried to save her statue from the
flames, perished in the attempt.

In October, 1391, the process of canonization was
concluded, and St. Bridget declared worthy to have
her name written in the Book of the Saints.
The ceremony is well described by Hammerich,[1]
from whom we will quote. He says that 'all the
bells in Rome rang to announce the good news
from the morning of the 6th of October and
during the night, and on the 7th the ceremony of
canonization was performed in the chapel of the
Vatican, because the Pope, Boniface IX., had an indis-
position which prevented him from holding the
function in St. Peter's Church. In the beautifully
decorated chapel, which was hung with gold-em-
broidered draperies for the august occasion, in the
presence of princes and nobles, the Pope, with a
patriarch on either side of him, and Cardinals bearing
the baldacchino over him, entered the chapel, and

[1] Hammerich, 'St. Birgitta,' p. 247.

Mass was celebrated. At the conclusion the Pope announced that the name of Bridget was to be inscribed among the saints, and he granted an indulgence to all who on that day and the following should honour her memory in St. Peter's or the Lateran. Then, as the Pope passed in procession through the chapel to his apartments in the Vatican, was heard for the first time the prayer, " Sancta Birgitta, ora pro nobis : Alleluia." '

The state of the Pope's health rendered it necessary to postpone the first High Mass, in honour of the new saint, until October the 8th, when it was celebrated in St. Peter's Church, which was decorated and illuminated for the occasion. After the High Mass was over the Pope was carried in procession to the open loggia, in front of the church, and there he opened the Golden Book, and taking a pen, wrote St. Bridget's name in it. A large crowd of people was present, to whom the Pope gave the solemn blessing. This canonization took place during the great schism, while the Papacy was claimed both by Boniface and the Antipope Clement VII., and the Scandinavian nations doubting in consequence whether it was valid, just before the close of the schism appealed to the Council of Constance, then sitting, for the ratification of the Act of Boniface. John XXIII., a doubtful Pope, was now the occupant of the chair of Peter, and he confirmed the Bull of canonization issued by Boniface IX., and also confirmed the Bulls approving of the Rule and Constitutions of the Order of St. Saviour. Finally, when the schism ceased, Martin V. again confirmed both the canonization and the Rule in 1419. Later on he placed all the Brigittine convents under the monastery of Vadstena, which until the Protestant Reformation remained the mother-house of this beautiful and most interesting Order.

Thus at last was accomplished the work for which so many persons had laboured so loyally; but, curious to say, none of the most active promoters of St. Bridget's cause lived to see it triumphantly ended. Besides Catherine, and Fathers Peter Olafson of Alvastra, Peter of Skening, and Gudmar, who were all dead, the saint's son Birger and her old friend, the saintly Bishop of Lincoping, Nicholas Hermanson, were also departed to join her in Paradise.

Over five hundred years have now elapsed since the great Swedish mystic lived, but one great work of her life, the establishment of the Order of St. Saviour, still survives, and from each of the four existing monasteries of Chudleigh, Altomünster, Weert and Uden, goes up the daily prayer that once more her daughters may return to their mother-house of Vadstena, now secularized and turned into an asylum and hospital.

If once that prayer be fulfilled, there will be hope of the conversion of Sweden, and perhaps, in the Providence of Almighty God, Vadstena may yet be destined to be in the future, as it was in the past, the centre of Catholicity in Scandinavia.

THE END

R. AND T. WASHBOURNE, LTD., 1, 2 AND 4, PATERNOSTER ROW, LONDON

CPSIA information can be obtained
at www.ICGtesting.com
Printed in the USA
LVOW09s1405081117
555501LV00012B/96/P

9 781298 403148